I LIKE TO START

with

SOMETHING FUNNY

DELIVER 100 TESTED, SHORT, CLEAN JOKES

2ND EDITION

MARK C. OVERTON

I Like to Start with Something Funny: Deliver 100 Tested, Short, Clean Jokes, 2nd Edition

Copyright © 2024 by Mark C. Overton

ISBN: 978-1962497534(sc)

ISBN: 978-1962497541(e)

The Reading Glass Books
1-888-420-3050
www.readingglassbooks.com
fulfillment@readingglassbooks.com

CONTENTS

DEDICATION

I dedicate this book to my wife, Margarita, whose contagious laugh cracks me up and brings side-splitting cackles, uncontrollable rolling-on-the-floor laughter, and a 'Happy' emoticon feeling. My wife keeps me smiling from ear to ear --Yas, Yas!

Simple Definition of Joke

: something said or done to cause laughter

: a brief story with a surprising and funny ending

: someone or something that is not worth taking seriously

Simple Definition of Laugh

: to show that you are happy or that you think something is funny by smiling and making a sound from your throat

: to think or say that someone or something is foolish and does not deserve serious attention or respect

: to not be bothered by something

CloseStyle: MLA APA Chicago

Top of Form

Bottom of Form

Source: Merriam-Webster's Learner's Dictionary

What's New in the Second Edition

I just wrote another book on how to fall down a staircase. It's a step-by-step guide -- LOL. This section also describes the specific updates, revisions, and additions made throughout the book.

In reflecting on the first edition of my book, I acknowledge that I was a beginning author at the time, and as a result, it may have needed to have the level of editing and polish I strive for in my writing. Since then, I have learned a great deal and improved as an author, and I am confident that the second edition has improved upon those shortcomings.

I could have included some grammatical errors or inconsistencies in the first edition. However, with the benefit of experience and feedback from readers like you, I have carefully reviewed and revised the content to enhance its overall quality and readability. To ensure that the second edition meets the high standards I set for myself as an author, I have also enlisted the help of professional editors.

The support and understanding you have shown me as I grow as a writer is greatly appreciated. Hopefully, the second edition will provide you with a more enjoyable reading experience, and you will find it an improvement over the first. Your feedback is invaluable, and I am always open to hearing your thoughts and suggestions to continue improving my work in future editions (See Review Ask).

Consequently, this section serves as a brief overview of the new edition. In this segment, you will find a summary of the changes, improvements, and updates made since the first edition. By reading this segment, you will also better understand what to expect and how the second edition differs from the previous one.

1. The second edition includes new information, research findings, or developments (See Appendix D). These updates will help you master and control your audience with witty, candid words of wisdom. As a public speaker, you can rise from mediocre to the most wanted.

2. Revisions and corrections: Accuracy is crucial for credibility. I have refined the text, clarified explanations, and corrected any errors or inconsistencies in the first edition. As a result, you'll master the art of creating a buzz in presentations and audiences – without losing control.

3. This second edition includes expanded chapters covering topics I needed to address adequately in the first edition. This inclusion helps provide a more comprehensive understanding of the subject matter. With this book, you can lead your crowd with witty words of wisdom that will awe them and keep them awake.

4. Enhanced graphics or illustrations: I improved the book's visual elements, including book parts and chapter images, to increase clarity and understanding. This medium enhances the way through which you share a story. You'll be able to bring back your crowd and presentation with these powerful words of witty wisdom.

5. Improved organization or structure: The second edition updates the chapter and append subtitles to enhance the flow of information, making it easier for you to navigate and comprehend. You'll find out how to become 'the audience magnet.' You'll discover how to steal the audience from the giant's den every time.

The second edition builds upon the foundation of the first, incorporating new information, improving clarity, and addressing any shortcomings. It seeks to provide readers with an updated and enhanced reading experience. Those who made a verified book purchase and were dissatisfied may receive this new edition – double the blessing! Thank you for joining me on this journey, and I hope you will find it a more refined and satisfying version of my book. From beginning to end, it offers a great mix of professionalism, inspiration, and humor. Similar to a book on anti-gravity I recently read, it's impossible to put down!

Unleashing the Power of a Simple Smile: A Currency of Connection

Mark C. Overton
5 December 2023

My greetings to you, Casey.

I hope this message finds you well. Do long speeches make you cringe and find yourself daydreaming instead of listening? Have you ever wished for a more engaging speaker? Are you looking to be an audience magnet or create an edge-of-the-seat experience when speaking publicly? Have you met people who brighten your day? Perhaps you've even heard the joke about the closing hymn. If this reminds you of one of your favorites, then you are an attentive listener. Your eagerness is evident. Before I share this joke with you, remember that every day is a gift from God. And if that doesn't excite you, what truly brings joy to your life?

As the preacher eagerly concluded his temperance sermon, he enthusiastically declared: "If I possessed all the beer, wine, whiskey, and demon rum in the world, I would toss it into the river!" The congregation responded with hearty affirmations. As he sat, the song leader rose uncertainly and suggested: "For our final hymn, let us sing #365: Shall We Gather at the River." Despite the fun of this moment, it was clear that the assembly took this issue seriously and eagerly anticipated their gathering at the river.

Brother, many individuals go through their day with a negative attitude and lack of enthusiasm. It is rare to see them smile or laugh. However, a simple smile holds great power in helping you connect with others. By smiling, you convey approachability, friendliness, and an openness to social interaction. This approach creates a positive and inviting atmosphere that lets people feel at ease and initiate conversations with you. Smiling is also contagious, as people reflect the emotions they see in others. As a result, by genuinely smiling, you can uplift those around you and facilitate meaningful connections and strong relationships. So, please do not underestimate the impact of a smile when forming genuine connections with people around you!

Rather than this, some individuals view everything as a burden. This style may lead to a sad demeanor, lack of excitement, or waking up in a lousy mood. There can be feelings of frustration, tension, annoyance, tension, or stress. Pessimists may trigger undesirable emotions. Self-esteem may be low, and the day may seem average. Despite working hard, having a good income, and being in good health, life can feel unfulfilling and empty, similar to consuming foods that offer no satisfaction or nourishment. Many activities fall into this category- initially enjoyable but ultimately causing feelings of self-disappointment.

Can you describe your current mental and emotional state? Are there any specific feelings or thoughts that dominate your experience? What factors may contribute to your lack of enjoyment in life, such as work, relationships, health, or other issues? Have any activities or hobbies that used to bring you joy stopped doing so? When was the last time you truly enjoyed something? Have you noticed any patterns or triggers that hinder your enjoyment in life? Do you struggle with negative thought patterns or behaviors? How would you rate your overall well-being and whether you physically and mentally care for yourself? Is there room for improvement in your self-care routine? Do you have someone to talk to about your feelings and a support system in place? Are there any people in your life who bring positivity and joy into it? Have you considered seeking professional help addressing these feelings of not enjoying life?

Sister, remember that God created us to experience joy and not to endure life with a long, hostile, discouraged, or grumpy face (see Appendix A and B).

While happiness may be temporary and dependent on circumstances, bliss is everlasting regardless of what we are going through. So, Casey, is your joy complete today? When something is full, there is no room for more. It is a feeling of complete fulfillment. What pleases you? Is it wine, women [men], or song (see Appendix C)? Whatever it may be, it takes you to your happy place. Whether it's through joyful songs, days, anniversaries, holidays, dances, meals, birthdays, endings, or New Year's celebrations, these bring us happiness. I have compiled witty anecdotes and laugh-out-loud jokes in this book to entertain, inspire, and uplift your audience.

With one touch of humor at a time, these words of wisdom strike a chord with the audience, bringing comfort to the masses. (Refer to Appendix D for more). This uplifting book serves as a guide for any speech. Use it as a blueprint to break the ice, engage, inspire, and encourage your listeners to absorb your message fully. The jokes will showcase your positive energy and give you an advantage while allowing room for improvisation, control, and ultimately winning over your audience. They also facilitate meaningful conversations and show support as your audience embarks on their journey toward finding joy in life again. Your spectators will undoubtedly laugh wholeheartedly and experience a happier life today!

Growing up in a church setting has given my family countless shared memories that we still laugh about today. These stories often remind me of Chris Rock's humorous quote about his siblings and our own experiences, such as my dad unplugging the clocks when we went to bed because we were poor. Despite any challenges, our family always found joy in each other's company, especially during dinner conversations sparked with nostalgia, like retelling the time my mama accidentally stepped in Wolfkin's poop. When I joined the United States Air Force, I also embraced the tradition of pranking recruits, adding to my list of hilarious family tales. Recently, my wife purchased a memorial tree to honor her late uncle and celebrate his life. His passing may have dimmed the world's light, but his "enjoying life" legacy will continue to shine through us. This story is just one example of how your family's experiences add depth and meaning to your ministry. Jesus understood the power of storytelling. God filled The Gospels with inspiring parables that convey essential moral and spiritual lessons. If Jesus recognized the effectiveness of using stories to communicate truth, we should follow his example. A well-crafted story captures people's interest and can help explain behaviors. It also allows you to apply biblical truths to everyday situations. However, it's worth noting that I don't intend for you to view these humorous anecdotes as doctrinal or theological; their purpose is to bring laughter to both the audience and the storyteller.

Moreover, faith-based stories are a powerful tool in proclaiming the gospel message. In John 9, we see Jesus healing a man who shared his faith story as evidence of a transformed life. You can better remember and retell God's Word by incorporating stories into your lives.

You can use stories to inspire and unite people of all ages, genders, cultures, and walks of life. You can also level the playing field for outsiders. You'll captivate listeners who would otherwise be unfamiliar with the Bible. You can communicate your truth more effectively if you use stories.

Likewise, these brief and humorous anecdotes have the potential to elicit personal experiences from your upbringing, church community, and global acquaintances. These narratives remind us of gratitude's immense impact on our perspective, even in difficult situations. You can nurture a grateful attitude by directing your attention towards the good things in life. You reflect your positive and faith-driven mindset in your uplifting, cheerful, and motivational messages that will brighten the day of those who come across them.

Who doesn't want a more joyful life? We all do. "I Like to Start with Something Funny" can help improve your life by providing over 100 reliable, clean, short jokes. These jokes will make you laugh whether you receive or send them. They serve as the perfect icebreaker and bring you and your audience joy. They can even glorify God and fulfill His purpose for creating us to enjoy life and experience unbridled pleasure. Let's explore the benefits of laughter and how it can positively impact you and your audience.

- Reduce your risk of strokes and heart attacks by lowering your blood pressure.
- Reduce stress hormone levels. Reduce anxiety and stress in your life.
- When you laugh, your stomach muscles expand and contract.
- Getting your heart pumping and burning calories is similar to strolling moderately.

- You can fight sickness by boosting your immune system cells.

- You can ease chronic pain by triggering the release of endorphins.

- A positive outlook on life will help you fight diseases more effectively.

In short, you'll gain—the benefits of the healing power of laughter, such as reducing stress, boosting the immune system, and improving cardiovascular health. You'll make people laugh and make them feel better. This happiness releases endorphins, elevating your mood and providing a sense of well-being. One customer purchased "I Like to Start with Something Funny" to assist her father in finding jokes for his Adult Sunday School class. He thoroughly enjoyed every joke she shared and praised them as "perfect for Sunday School" and "great short jokes to enjoy." Another satisfied buyer said these were "clean jokes perfect for seniors with Alzheimer's." She read them to her mother daily, resulting in frequent laughter from both of them. She declared it the best $5 she had spent in a long time. With such positive reviews, "I Like to Start with Something Funny" could also answer your prayers. Research findings and developments related to these topics include:

- Laughter therapy, or laughter yoga, involves intentional laughter exercises that can promote physical and emotional well-being. Children laugh 200 times daily, and adults laugh 14 times daily. According to studies, it reduces anxiety and depression and improves quality of life in general.

- •Positive psychology focuses on understanding human well-being. Researchers emphasize the importance of positive emotions, including laughter, in enhancing overall well-being. It examines factors that contribute to happiness and fulfillment.

- Social interactions also benefit from laughter. In various social settings, researchers showed laughter to improve communication, increase trust, and create a positive atmosphere. It helps strengthen relationships, promotes social bonding, and enhances group cohesion.

- It emphasizes the importance of finding joy in God, cultivating gratitude, and seeking contentment in all circumstances, but not specifically about laughter. In these teachings, believers are encouraged to pursue happiness through a spiritual lens.

By utilizing the guidance in this inspirational book, you can enhance your chances of tapping into your inner comedian and becoming a sought-after speaker. With over 100 tried-and-tested, clean jokes, you can create an exciting and enjoyable experience for your audience. This book is a valuable resource for any speech, offering a blueprint for captivating your listeners and delivering impactful messages. These jokes also serve as an effective tool for initiating meaningful discussions and bringing more laughter and joy into people's lives. Take advantage of the opportunity to become the speaker everyone wants to hear by using these powerful techniques. Whether reading these amusing stories or sharing them with your audience, these short, clean jokes will make everyone laugh. Also, see Appendix D. Double the fun, double the joy! As believers, folks expect us to radiate true happiness instead of faking it. People may wonder why we are so joyful and even question if we are under the influence – lots of laughs. But as faithful Christians, we know this comes from living a dedicated life for our Lord. Let's take it further and spread your joy wherever you go, brightening others' days with a simple smile. Remember, "This is the day that the Lord has made; let us rejoice and be glad in it" (Ps. 118:24). So go ahead and share your joy with others - after all, it doesn't cost anything but yields excellent returns. And don't waste time doubting yourself; your happiness will surely return to you.

When reading for spiritual growth, expect to start your day in faith. These enlightening jokes will bring strength and happiness and make your day enjoyable, like a beloved song or hymn. They can uplift and guide you through tough times, similar to a choir's role in church. These edifying jokes help bring the Spirit into your life and keep you connected to God while having fun. As a speaker, you'll learn the sequential process of telling a funny joke, including framing, speaking, and responding -- known as The Humor Exchange. This dynamic method involves an interactive exchange of laughter and enjoyment between the joke teller and the audience, much like the main parts of a speech and attending church.

- Framing: opening (church invitation),
- Telling: body (friend attends church) and
- Responding: conclusion (pastor seals the deal).

When we dig deeper into this arrangement, Casey, it becomes evident that humor is a powerful weapon in the speaker's arsenal, especially if they're naturally funny. The enriching joke adds significance to the message, event, people, and speaker, while the elevating joke is separate from what you are trying to accomplish; people can concentrate on the message.

Framing: Unhappiness Occurring Every Day

Starting with an upbeat joke in your message can make a lasting impact on your audience's memory. It is no secret that the beginning of a speech is crucial in capturing attention and setting a favorable tone for communication. Research shows that the average attention span is only 8 seconds, so engaging and grabbing your audience's attention is essential. This opening is where short, clean jokes can effectively keep your high-energy audience focused and interested. Think of it as an icebreaker, instantly grabbing the interest of your limited-time witnesses before diving into the main presentation. In this way, the joke acts like a friendly church greeter, welcoming visitors and attendees with a smile at the door. Like this role, the lighthearted joke sets the tone for the entire presentation as it personifies and represents you as the speaker.

Similarly, when it comes to persuading, inspiring, or influencing your fans (e.g., 'stans' – stalker fans), a priceless joke as your opening (i.e., punchline closer) is by far the most crucial moment of your delivery. This entertaining quip contributes to the concept of recency, making you more memorable to viewers who will strongly recall what you say at the end. Are you following me? This humorous approach not only lightens the mood and creates an immediate bond but also gets viewers hyped and on your side. As a result, they are more likely to tune in and become receptive to your topic. By reducing tension and providing showbiz value, your jolly joke establishes that you are human and allows spectators to identify with you. Plus, it lets everyone in the room have fun and share a laugh.

As a follower [of Christ], your good-hearted joke can also break the ice for hungry parishioners to hear the Good News; you first enlighten your listeners with gentle humor. As a bonus, these funny jokes enhance an opportunity to share God's love through Christ and set the tone for the upcoming worship service or Sunday School lesson.

Telling: Short, Clean Jokes that Break the Ice and Grab the Audience's Attention

After setting the stage with a good-natured joke, you can begin your lesson on a light note. This approach will convey a conversational tone and show your audience you are relatable. Your constant positive outlook will shine through as you effortlessly share anecdotes that will have your viewers laughing. And rest assured, your punchlines will stay strong. No matter what type of presentation you're giving, whether a class or a sermon, those listening will see you as a source of humor. I promise I'm not exaggerating. Your listeners will receive your jokes well. You'll always come across as upbeat and humorous, whether delivering them to your glee club or any other setting. Do you like to make people laugh or break the ice in meetings or presentations? No problem. You won't bomb on stage or face adverse reactions like heckling or booing. Your crowd won't see these lighthearted jokes as offensive or outdated – no one will disapprove of you. Instead, they'll boost your confidence and bring joy through laughter. Trust me, these good-natured jokes will not result in awkward moments or embarrass you. I guarantee satisfaction when sharing them with your loved ones, colleagues, and acquaintances.

Keep the faith, and you'll witness great things come to life. You have the potential to be at the top and take advantage of opportunities while they're hot! You've got this. Start as an underdog and emerge as a champion; these lighthearted jokes will surely resonate with your loved ones and elicit a positive response! Just like the 5 "Bs" of a presentation - Be Brief Brother (or Baby), Be Brief - that's the beauty of these short, clean jokes. They help maintain a concise and engaging atmosphere in your laugh shack! What do I mean? As an icebreaker, they give you a boost and support King Henry VIII's famous words to each of his seven wives, "I won't keep you long." With your natural gift for storytelling, you'll be cracking up and having a joyful day; you'll be on cloud nine and thoroughly enjoying yourself. Your crew will also appreciate the humor and find it hilarious; they'll understand it and laugh until their sides hurt! Ha ha!

Responding to Short, Clean Jokes to Encourage Laughter and Bring Joy

After telling your humdinger joke, you hope for a response of laughter from your audience. You want them to understand and find it funny, as the ultimate goal is to make them laugh out loud. People say that whoever laughs last didn't fully comprehend the joke. This ties into using a slapstick joke as a closing punchline, which invites others to join in or consider your message. This invitation emphasizes the importance of starting with something funny. The impact of a playful joke, whether delivered by a presenter or yourself, is crucial in making participants see the humorous side and fully appreciate it. This book will serve as a beacon of God's kindness, spreading His message of joy to all. Whether faced with challenges or in moments of pure happiness, these hysterical jokes will leave you in stitches and bring a constant smile to your face. Your expression is your most valuable accessory, and reading these witty jokes can be likened to giving a powerful speech - an 'opening' that invites others to church, a 'body' where a friend joins you, and an inspiring 'conclusion' delivered by a passionate preacher.

Let's jump right into unleashing your inner comedian and becoming the highly sought-after speaker you want to be today! The opportunity is knocking, and it's up to you to answer. Don't hesitate; those in the know will snatch up these tried and true, clean, and concise jokes. You can read "I Like to Start with Something Funny" without distractions on this platform, creating a more immersive experience filled with entertainment and knowledge. While waiting for this book is well worth it, sharing or reading these tested jokes provides immediate satisfaction. To fully reap the benefits of this book, I organized it into two sections - Spiritual Joy and Non-spiritual Humor- allowing you to navigate and recollect critical points easily.

Presenters have proved these actual short jokes effective. Each chapter quickly identifies the protagonist who becomes the subject of the zinger, making it easy to select your perfect joke to deliver to your audience. The table of contents makes navigating a breeze, giving you an edge in choosing the best-fit joke for your crowd. Trust me, they're a quick read! And the ending will leave you wanting more. These jokes will liven up any dull day and entertain you and your gathering. You'll become hooked on these clean anecdotes for personal growth and enjoyment. And don't worry, I didn't fill them with offensive or cringe-worthy content. That's not what I'm about. Your gathering will have everyone in stitches, their cheeks aching from laughter and feeling pleasantly amused. They may even compliment you with a playful "You're so crazy!" (or "cray-cray" for the slang-inclined). And once you reach the end of the book, you won't want to let it go. Take this cherished book wherever you go – at home, work, or on the move. Some might argue that it brings more joy than sex itself. You'll have the bonus of reliving these clever jokes repeatedly. These little nuggets of humor are timeless and effortless. Trust me, this is no joke (pun intended). By following the formula I reveal in this book, you can effortlessly deliver these clean and safe jokes that will have everyone laughing or blushing. In this introduction, I hope you know what "I Like to Start with Something Funny" is about. Specifically, how to structure a joke through its opening, body, and conclusion – just like a speech or a church service would have its set parts – "invitation," "attendance," and "seal of approval" from the pastor. These carefree jokes will create a fantastic first impression for your audience in all facets of their life. You're all set to dive into this book and find humor wherever possible. I wrote this book to give you that freedom. However, if you're eager to get started with the witty jokes, head straight to Chapter 1 – that's where the non-stop laughter begins! Enjoy your reading experience as much as a pig wallowing in mud or someone on a Friday evening after work! Laugh out loud!

PART I.

SPIRITUAL JOY
Soulful Bliss: Embracing the Divine Delight

MALE WISECRACKS
Cracking the Code: Unraveling the Wit and Humor of Men

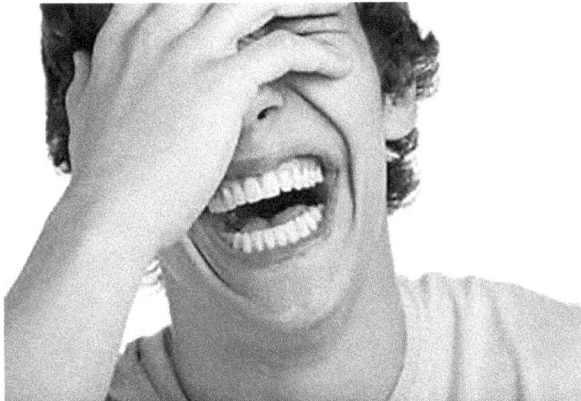

I like to start with something funny. I heard about this man. He called the church office and said, "I want to speak to the 'head hog at the trough.'" The secretary was offended. She said, 'If you mean the pastor, you're going to have to call him Pastor, but you may not call him the head hog at the trough.' He said, 'Well, I was thinking about donating five thousand dollars to your church. She said, 'Hang on, Porky just walked in.'

I like to start with something funny. I heard about this man. He came up to a Baptist pastor. He said, Sir, my dog just passed away. Could you come to my house and have a funeral for him? The pastor seemed annoyed and said Naw, I can't do a funeral for a dog. The man said, 'That's too bad;

I was thinking about donating five thousand dollars to your church.' The pastor smiled and said, 'Why didn't you tell me your dog was Baptist.'

I like to start with something funny. I heard about this minister who was driving down the road. He looked down and accidentally veered off, went through a ditch, and crashed into a telephone pole. The man behind him pulled over and ran to him, 'Sir, are you okay?' The minister said, 'Yes, I'm fine; the angel of the Lord was with me.'

I like to start with something funny. I heard about these three men who were out hiking through the wilderness. They encountered this violent river and needed to get to the other side. The first man prayed, "Please, God give me the strength to make it across." And Poof! God gave him big arms and strong legs; he could swim across in 2 hours. Seeing this, the next man said, "God, please give me the strength and the tools I need to make it across." And Poof! God gave him a boat. He was able to row across in 30 minutes. The next man said, "God give me the strength, the tools, and the intelligence to make it across." And Poof! God turned him into a woman. She looked at the map, hiked 5 minutes upstream, and then walked across the bridge. The man shook his head and said, 'You'd better let him ride with me; you're about to kill him."

I like to start with something funny. I heard about this pastor. He decided to skip church one Sunday morning and play golf. He told his assistant he wasn't feeling well, and he drove to a golf course in another city where nobody would know him. He teed off on the first hole, and suddenly, the wind picked up his ball. And carried it an extra 100 yards and blew it right into the hole -- for a 420-yard hole-in-one. An angel looked at God and said, "What you do that for?" God smiled and said, "Who is he going to tell."

I like to start with something funny. I heard about this pastor. He was raising money for a new sanctuary. He told his congregation one Sunday morning, "If anybody will give a thousand dollars, you can pick out the next three hymns." A little old lady in the back raised her hand and said, "Pastor, I will do it." He was so excited he said, "Thank you so much. Go ahead and pick out the next three hymns." She looked over the congregation and said, "I take Him, Him and Him."

I like to start with something funny. I heard about this minister. He brought a new horse. He trained it to respond to 'Praise the Lord,' meaning 'giddy up,' and 'Hallelujah,' meaning 'Whoa.' Every time he said, "Praise the Lord," the horse ran. When he said, "Whoa," it would quickly stop. One day, he was out riding. The horse got spooked and took off straight toward the cliff --running at full speed. In the panic, he couldn't remember what he trained the horse to respond to. He said, "Bless God," "Glory," "Amen." Nothing happened. At the last second, he shouted "Hallelujah." The horse came to a screeching halt just inches before the cliff's edge. He breathed a sigh of relief and said, "Praise the Lord."

I like to start with something funny. I heard about this atheist. He was spending a quiet day on the lake. Then, all of a sudden, his boat was attacked by the Loch Ness Monster. One easy flip tossed him and his vessel high into the air. Then it opened its mouth, waiting to swallow as the man tumbled head over heels. He cried out, "God help me." All at once, time stood still. The whole picture froze. God said, "But I didn't think you believed in me." The atheist said, "God, please give me a break. I didn't believe in the Loch Ness Monster two minutes ago, either."

I like to start with something funny. I heard about this pastor. He found a small box hidden in his wife's closet. He opened it up. There were six eggs and a 1000-dollar bill. He asked his wife about it. She explained how she put an egg in the box whenever he preached a lousy sermon. After 35 years of ministering, he felt pretty good about himself -- only six bad sermons. He asked, "What was the $1000?" She said, "Every time I got a dozen eggs, I sold them for a dollar."

I like to start with something funny. I heard about this pastor. He parked in a 'No Parking' zone downtown in a large city. He left a note on the windshield, saying, "Officer, I circled this block ten times. If I don't park here, I'll miss my appointment." In big letters, he wrote, "FORGIVE US OF OUR TREPASSES." He returned to his car and had a ticket. The officer had written him a note. It said, "Sir, I circled this block for ten years. I could lose my job if I don't give you a ticket." In big letters, he wrote, "LEAD US NOT INTO TEMPTATIONS."

I like to start with something funny. I heard about this pastor. Close friends asked him to inform a member of his congregation, who had a heart condition, that he had just inherited 10 million dollars. They were concerned because of the shock that he may have a heart attack. The pastor said, "Sir, what would you do if you inherited 10 million dollars?" The man said, "Pastor, I'll first give half of it to the church." At that point, the pastor fell over dead.

I like to start with something funny. I heard about this minister. He was walking down the street. He came upon this group of young boys surrounding a small dog. He asked what they were doing. They explained they were having a contest. And whoever could tell the biggest lie would get to keep the dog. The minister launched a 10-minute sermon on lying, starting with, Don't you know lying is a sin? And ending with when I was your age, I never told a lie. There was complete silence. When he thought he had gotten through to them, the youngest boy said, "Alright, give him the dog."

I like to start with something funny. I heard about this minister. He was driving down the road when a policeman pulled him over. The officer came up to the window and smelled alcohol. He saw a thermos and said, "Sir, what are you drinking?" The minister said, "Just water officer." He asked to see the thermos, took one sniff, and said, "Smells like wine to me." The minister said, "What do you know? Jesus did it again."

I like to start with something funny. I heard about these three pastors. They were in a boat on a lake, fishing one day together. One said, "We never get to let our hair down." Let's each tell the area we struggle in the most -- our greatest sin so we can pray for each other. The first man said, "I hate to admit this, but I have a problem with gambling. I sneak out a lot of nights and go gamble." The second pastor said, "I'm ashamed to admit this, but I have a problem cheating. I hardly ever pay my taxes." The third pastor sat there silently. They waited and waited. He wouldn't budge. They said, "We're not getting off this boat until you tell us your greatest sin." He said, "My greatest sin is gossiping, and I can't wait to get off this boat."

I like to start with something funny. I heard about this pastor. He was raising money for a new sanctuary. He told his congregation, "I got good news and bad news. The good news is we have plenty of money for our new sanctuary. The bad news is it's still in your pockets.

I like to start with something funny. I heard about this Baptist man named Bill. He likes to sneak out to the horse races and bet. One day, after losing almost all his money, he saw a Catholic priest step onto the track and bless a horse. Sure enough, that horse won first place. In the next race, he blessed another horse, and that horse won again. Seeing this, Bill went to the ATM and took out all his money. This time, he saw the priest touch the horse's forehead, eyes, ears, and legs. Feeling confident, he bet all his money. But in the middle of that race, the horse fell dead. He couldn't believe it. He said to the priest, "What in the world happened?" He said, "That's the problem with you Protestants. You don't know the difference between a blessing and the Last Rites."

I like to start with something funny. I heard about this minister. He was up on the pulpit preaching away one Sunday morning when he noticed a man on the front row sound asleep. That made him so aggravated he started preaching louder and more demanding. But it seemed like the louder he got, the sounder he slept. So, he finally stopped in the middle of his sermon and said to the man sitting next to him, "Would you please wake that man up?" The man said, "Wake him up yourself. You put him to sleep."

I like to start with something funny. One Sunday morning, this man walked into church wearing blue jeans, a t-shirt, and an old cowboy hat. Some of the members were appalled. They sent notes to the Pastor expressing their concern. Afterward, the Pastor told the man he needed to pray. And ask God what he should wear when he returns to his church. The following week, the man came back wearing the same thing. Pastor said, "I told you to ask God what you should wear before you return to my church." The man said, "I did ask God, and He told me He didn't know what to wear because He has never been here before."

I like to start with something funny. I heard about this pastor. He was in the lobby after service, greeting people. He saw this man he hadn't seen in a long time. I pulled him over and said, "Sir, you must join the Army of the Lord." The man said, "What are you talking about? I'm in the Army of the Lord." The pastor said, "How come I only see you on Christmas and Easter?" He whispered back, "I'm in the Secret Service."

I like to start with something funny. I heard about this minister. He was driving down the road when a policeman pulled him over. The officer came up to the window and smelled alcohol. He saw a thermos and said, "Sir, What are you drinking?" The minister said, "Just water officer." He asked to see the thermos, took one sniff, and said, "Smells like wine to me." The minister said, "What you know, Jesus did it again."

I like to start with something funny. I heard about this minister who died. He was standing in line at the Pearly Gates, and in front of him was a man dressed in a loud shirt, wearing blue jeans and sunglasses. Saint Peter asked, "What's your name, sir?" He said, "My name is Joe Cohen, a taxicab driver, New York City." Peter checked his list, handed him a gold staff and a silk robe, and said, "Welcome to Heaven." The minister said, "I'm Reverend Joseph Snow, Pastor of Saint Mary's Cathedral." Peter checked his list and handed him a cotton robe and a wooden staff. He said, "Hey, wait a minute. That's not fair. The taxicab driver got a gold staff and a silk robe. How could that be?" Peter said, "Sir, up here, we work by results. When you preached, people slept. But when he drove, people prayed."

I like to start with something funny. I heard about this elderly minister. He was close to death. He sent word for two of his members, an IRS agent, and a lawyer, to come to his house. Upon arrival, he motioned for them to sit on each side of the bed. The men were very moved that they could be with the minister in his final moment. [At] one point, the lawyer asked sincerely, "Sir, why did you choose us?" The minister mustered strength and said, "Jesus died between two sinners. That's the way I want to go."

I like to start with something funny. I heard about this wealthy man who was known for being eccentric. He was having a big party at this house, and in his backyard, he had a huge pool filled with alligators and sharks. He told the guests, "Anyone that will swim across my pool, I'll give you anything you want." There was a big splash in a few minutes, and a man was in there going 90 to nothing, dodging alligators and maneuvering around the sharks. He made it to the other side just in the nick of time and got out as frantic as can be. The wealthy man said, "I can't believe you're the bravest person I've ever met. Now, what is it that you would want?" The man said, "What I want, more than anything else, is the name of the person who pushed me in."

I like to start with something funny. I heard about this man. He was driving through an intersection that authorities monitored with cameras. If you ran the light or broke the law in any way, it would take your picture, and you would receive a ticket in the mail. So, he made sure to go through it extra slowly and not break any laws. But he noticed the camera flashed and took his picture. He thought that's not right. He turned around and drove through it again -- even more slowly. Once again, it took his picture. He thought they messed up this thing; they could not give me a ticket. Out of spite, he drove through it three more times. Each time, he waved at the camera with a big smile. A week later, he received five tickets for not wearing his seatbelt.

I like to start with something funny. I heard about these three men: a Baptist, a Catholic, and a Charismatic. They died on the same day and went to heaven. St Peter met them at the gates and said, "I'm sorry, men, your rooms are unavailable yet." He didn't know what to do. He decided to call Satan and see if he would keep them for a little while. Satan reluctantly agreed. A few hours later, Satan called back and said, 'Peter, you got to get these guys. The Baptist man is saving everybody. The Catholic man is forgiving everybody, and the Charismatic has already raised enough money for air conditioning.'

I like to start with something funny. I heard about this man who died and went to heaven. St Peter escorted him down this long hallway filled with clocks. The hands on the clocks were all moving at different speeds. Peter explained that every person has a clock. When they sin, the clock ticks. The man saw a clock verily moving. It was Billy Graham's clock. There was another clock creeping along -- Mother Teresa's clock. He said curiously, 'Can I see my clock?' Peter said, "We keep yours in the office and use it as a fan."

I like to start with something funny. I heard about these two guys. They argued for years on whether Jesus was white or whether he was black. Archie was sure he was white. Jack was just as sure he was black. As faith would have it, they both died on the same day. They rushed to the Pearly Gates. Said St Peter, 'Please tell us, is Jesus white or black?' We've been arguing our whole life over this. About that time, Jesus walked up and said, "Buenas Dias."

I like to start with something funny. I heard about a man walking through the woods with a friend. All of a sudden, they came up on this giant grizzly bear. They froze in their tracks. As the bear intently stared them down. They contemplated what they should do. The man turned to his friend and said, 'I think we should run.' His friend said, 'Are you crazy? You can't outrun a grizzly bear.' He said, "I know that. I don't have to outrun him; I must outrun you."

I like to start with something funny. I heard about this man that was walking on the beach. God said, "Son, you've been so faithful. I will grant you one special wish". He was so excited. He said, "God, I always wanted to go to Hawaii, but I'm afraid to fly. So I wish that You would build me a bridge across the ocean". God said, "Son, that is impossible. Think of the logistics of that. Now take some time and wish again". He said, "Okay, God, I have been married four times. All my ex-wives say I am so insensitive. So, my wish is that I would be able to understand a woman. I want to know why they think like they think. Why do they feel like they feel." There was a long pause. God said, "Do you want two or four lanes on that bridge?"

I like to start with something funny. I heard about this older man. He had a severe hearing problem for years and years. He could hardly hear anything. One day, he went to the doctor, and they fitted him with a new hearing aid to listen to 100 percent. A month later, he went back for a checkup. The doctor said, "Man, your family must be happy, your hearing is perfect." He said, "No, I haven't told my family. I listen to the conversations and change my will three times."

I like to start with something funny. I heard about this man. He was sitting in a dark restaurant. He asked the lady beside him, "Would you like to hear a 'Blond' joke." She said, "Well, before you tell me, you should know I'm blond, six foot tall, and a professional bodybuilder. The lady beside me is blond, six foot two, and a professional wrestler. And the lady next to her is blond, six foot five, and the world's kickboxing champion." "Now, do you still want to tell me?" He thought about it momentarily and said, "Naw, not if I'm going to have to explain it three times."

I like to start with something funny. I heard about this 92-year-old man. He wasn't feeling well one day, so he decided to go to the doctor for a checkup. A few days later, the doctor saw him walking down the street with a beautiful young lady by his side. And he seemed to be just as happy as could be. The Doctor was surprised. He said, "Wow, you sure are doing much better." The man said, "Yes, Doctor, I just took your orders. You said to get a hot momma and stay cheerful." The Doctor said, "I didn't say that! I said you got a heart murmur. Be careful!"

I like to start with something funny. I heard a young man asking God, "How long was a million years to Him?" God said, "A million years to Me was like a second in your time." The young man asked God, "What was a million dollars to Him?" God said, "A million dollars to Me was like a single penny to you." The young man gathered his courage and asked God, "Would you please give me a penny?" God said, "Sure, just a second."

I like to start with something funny. I heard about this pastor. He was new in town. He went door to door, inviting people to come to his church. He knocked on this one door. He could tell someone was there, but nobody would answer. He took his church card out and wrote on the back the Scripture reference, "REVELATION 3:20," and left it on the door. The following Sunday after service, an usher handed him the same card under what he had written was the Scripture reference: "GENESIS 3:10." Here's what they say: The pastor's word, Revelation 3:20, "Behold I stand at the door and knock. If anyone answers, I will come in." The reply was Genesis 3:10: "I heard your voice, but I was afraid because I was naked."

I like to start with something funny. I heard a young man asking God, "How long was a million years to Him?" God said, "A million years to Me was like a single second to him." The young man asked God, "What was a million dollars to Him?" God said, "A million dollars to Me was like a single penny to him." The young man gathered his courage and asked God, "Would you please give me a penny?" God said, "Just a second."

I like to start with something funny. I heard about this atheist. He was spending a quiet day on the lake. Then, all of a sudden, his boat was attacked by the Loch Ness Monster. One easy flip tossed him and his vessel high into the air. Then it opened its mouth, waiting to swallow as the man tumbled head over heels. He cried out, "God help me." All at once, time stood still. The whole picture froze. God said, "But I didn't think you believed in me." The atheist said, "God, please give me a break. I didn't believe in the Loch Ness Monster two minutes ago, either."

I like to start with something funny. One day, God told the men in heaven, "I want you to form two lines." One line is for the men who are the head of the house. The other line is for the men who let the woman be the head of the house. The line where the woman ran the house was 100 miles long. There was only one man in the other line. God said, "Men, I'm ashamed of you. I created you to be the head, but only one man stood up to make me proud." He looked at him and said, "Son, tell them how you managed to be the only one in this line?" The man looked confused and said, "I don't know. My wife told me to stand here."

I like to start with something funny. I heard about this blond person. They were so blond that they tripped over a cordless phone. They were so blond that they asked for a price check at the 'Dollar Store.' They were so blond that it took them two hours to watch '60 Minutes'. They were so blond that they thought 'Taco Bell' was the Mexican phone company.

I like to start with something funny. I heard about this man. He was the only Protestant in a large Catholic neighborhood. While his neighbors ate cold fish every Friday during Lent, he grilled a steak in the backyard. They couldn't stand the temptation and decided to try to convert him to Catholicism. He finally agreed. The priest sprinkled water over him and said, "You were born a Baptist; you were raised a Baptist. Now you're a Catholic." The following year, on the first Friday of Lent, they smelled the same smell in the air. They rushed to his house. He was in the backyard sprinkling water over this steak, saying, "You were born a cow; you were raised a cow, but now you're a fish."

I like to start with something funny. I heard about this man named Bubba. He lived way out in the country. There was this stray dog that kept showing up at his house. His wife said, "Bubba, you have to put the dog in the truck, take him out to the woods, and drop him off. That's where he lives." Bubba drove him a mile down the road [and] dropped him off. When he returned home, the dog walked up the driveway and practically beat him. He did the same thing; it happened again. His wife said, "Bubba, you have to take him way out, drive him around in circles [and] get him all mixed up." Bubba drove him an hour away, crisscrossed country roads he had never gone before [and] dropped the dog off. Two hours later, Bubba called his wife from the truck and said, "Did that dog make it back home?"

29

She said, "Yeah, here he comes walking up." He said, "Do me a favor, [and] put him on the phone. I need directions."

I like to start with something funny. I heard about this 85-year-old man. He was fishing one day and listened to this voice saying, "Pick me up." He looked around, saw nothing, and thought he was dreaming. Then he heard it again, "Pick me up." He looked down and saw a frog on the ground. He said in amazement, "Are you talking to me?" The frog said, "Yes, pick me up and kiss me, and I'll turn into a beautiful bride." He quickly picked the frog up and put it in his front pocket. The frog said, "Hey! What are you doing? I said kiss me, and I'll become a beautiful bride." The man said, "No thanks. At my age, I'd rather have a talking frog.

I like to start with something funny. I heard about these three men traveling together: a Hindu priest, a Jewish Rabbi, and a Televangelist. They stopped at a farmhouse for lodging, and the farmer said, "I only have room for two in the house. Someone's going to have to stay in the barn." The Hindu priest said, "I'll do it." After a few minutes, there was a knock on the door. He said, "I can't stay out there. There's a cow, and cows are sacred in our religion." The Jewish Rabbi said, "I'll do it." After a few minutes, there was a knock on the door. He said, "I can't stay out there. There's a pig, and that wouldn't be Kosher." The Televangelist finally said, "Alright, I'll do it." In a few minutes, there was a knock on the door. It was the cow and the pig.

I like to start with something funny. I heard about this man at the airline ticket counter, hollering and screaming at the agent for being so rude. As he continued to rant and rave, the agent was just as calm and polite as possible. She treated him so respectfully like it didn't even bother her. He left, and the next man stepped up and said, "Wow! I am so impressed. You must be a Christian. How could you possibly be so kind to him?" She smiled and said, "Aww, it wasn't that hard. He's going to Detroit, but his bags are going to Bangkok."

I like to start with something funny. I heard about this single man. He had been living at home with his elderly father, who was very wealthy. The son decided he needed to find a wife to enjoy the fortune he would inherit when his father died. One evening at an investment meeting, he saw the most beautiful girl he had ever seen. She took his breath away. He told her, "I look like just an ordinary guy. But in a few years, when my father passes, I will inherit hundreds of millions of dollars. Impressed, she took his business card. Three months later, she married his father.

I like to start with something funny. I heard about this senior citizen. He was driving down the freeway in his brand-new Corvette with the top down, going 80 miles per hour, when he saw flashing red lights from a state trooper in his rearview mirror. He floored it and took off at 100 miles an hour without thinking about it. He heard the sirens behind him. He finally pulled over and said, "Officer, I'm so sorry. I don't know what I was thinking." The state trooper said, "Listen, it's Friday, 4 o'clock [and] my shift is over in 30 minutes. If you tell me why you're speeding that I've never heard before, I'll let you go." The man thought about it and said, "Officer, years ago, my wife ran off with a state trooper, and I thought you were bringing her back." The officer said, "Have a great weekend!"

I like to start with something funny. I heard about a man who tried to sell his vacuum because it was just collecting dust. Let's not let our dreams collect dust, let's put them into action!

I like to start with something funny. I heard about a man who was struggling with a difficult situation in his life. The man explained his worries to the doctor, saying, "Doctor, I'm going through a tough time. I feel overwhelmed, stressed, and anxious. I don't know how to find peace." The doctor listened carefully and then handed the man a prescription. Surprised, the man asked, "Is this some kind of medication to help me calm down?" The doctor smiled and replied, "No, it's not medication. It's a prescription for gratitude." The doctor went on to explain that when we focus on the things, we're grateful for, it can shift our perspective and bring more peace into our lives. The man took the prescription to heart and began practicing gratitude daily. Over time, he noticed a significant change in his outlook, and his worries faded.

I like to start with something funny. I once heard a story about a man who asked God for a bike, but then realized that's not how God works. So, he stole a bike and asked God for forgiveness. Remember, it's better to seek God's guidance and trust His plan!"

31

Chapter 2

FEMALE QUIPS

Fierce and Fabulous: Unleashing the Power of Female Wit and Banter

Ilike to start with something funny. I heard about this elderly lady. She came into church one Sunday morning. A friendly usher greeted her. 'Mam, where would you like to sit?' She said, "I would like to sit in the front row." 'Oh No, Mam, you don't want to do that; our pastor is very boring. He will put you to sleep; let me seat you somewhere else.' She was appalled. She said, 'Sir, do you know who I am.' He said, 'No.' She said, 'I'm the pastor's mother.' He hung his head in embarrassment. Finally, he looked up and said, "Mam, do you know who I am?" She said, "'No." He said, "Thank God."

I like to start with something funny. I heard about this elderly lady. At the store, she accidentally locked her keys in her car. With no success, she used a coat hanger to open it. She prayed and asked God to help her. About this time, this rough-looking guy drove up on a motorcycle. He was wearing leather, tattoos, and a skull cap. In 15 seconds, he had her car door open. She hugged him and said, 'Lord, thank you for sending me this nice man.' He said, "Lady, I'm not a nice man. I just got out of prison for auto theft.' She hugged him more and said, "Lord, thank you, you even sent me a Professional."

I like to start with something funny. I heard about this elderly lady who was close to death. She had never been married. She called her pastor over to talk about her funeral. She said that she only wanted female pallbearers. The pastor looked at her strangely and asked, "Why?" She said, "The men wouldn't take me out when I was alive. They're not going to take me out when I'm dead."

I like to start with something funny. I heard about this group of elderly ladies. Way up in their eighties, they were driving down the freeway together when they got pulled up by a police officer. The officer said to the woman driving, "Mam, Do you realize you're only going 35 miles an hour?" She said, "Yes, officer, I realize that." He said, "Why are you going so slow?" She said, "That's what the sign said." He laughed and said, "No, mam, that's the number of the freeway. This interstate is Highway 35." By the way, "Why are these women so terrified?" She smiled and said, "We just got off Highway 95."

I like to start with something funny. I heard about this elderly lady. She came into church one Sunday morning, and a friendly usher greeted her and said, "Ma'am, where would you like to sit?" She said, "I would like to sit in the front row." And he said, "Oh no, ma'am, you don't want to do that. Our pastor is very boring. He'll put you to sleep. Let me seat you somewhere else." She was appalled. She said, "Sir, do you know who I am?" He said, "No." She said, "I am the Pastor's Mother." He hung his head in embarrassment, and finally, he looked up and said, "Ma'am, do you know who I am." She said, "No." He said, "Thank God."

I like to start with something funny. I heard about this 84-year-old woman. She went on a blind date with a 93-year-old man. When she returned home to her daughter's house, she seemed upset. Her daughter asked her, "What was wrong?" She said, "I had to slap him three times." She said, "You mean he tried to get fresh." She said, "Naw, I thought he was dead."

I like to start with something funny. I heard about this 85-year-old woman. She went on a blind date with a 92-year-old man. She came home very frustrated, and her daughter said, "Mom, what's wrong?" She said, "I had to slap him three times." The daughter said, "You mean he tried to get fresh?" She said, "No, I thought he was dead."

I like to start with something funny. I heard about this 84-year-old woman. She'd gotten out of shape and knew she needed to start exercising. So, she decided to join an aerobics class for seniors. On the first day, she bent, twisted, gyrated back and forth, jumped up and down, and sweated for over an hour. But she said the class was over by the time she got her leotards on.

I like to start with something funny. I heard about these sisters, ages 96, 94, and 92, who lived together. One day, the 96-year-old draws a bath. She puts one foot in and stops. She hollers downstairs, "I can't remember if I was getting in or out." The 94-year-old said, "Just a second, I will come up and help you." She gets halfway up the stairs and stops. She said, "I can't remember if I was going up or coming down." The 92-year-old nodded and said, "Boy, I hope I never get that forgetful." She knocked on wood for good luck. [... the sound of knocking on wood]. She said, "Hang on, I'll help both of you as soon as I see who's at the door.

I like to start with something funny. I heard about this grandmother who lived in the country. She'll go out on her front porch every morning and thank the Lord for another day. Her neighbor didn't believe in God. He'll shout back: "There's no such thing as the Lord." One day, he overheard asking God to give her groceries for the week. He snuck over the following day and put some groceries on her front porch. She rose and said, "Thank you, Lord, you did it again!" He laughed and laughed and said, "God didn't give you those groceries. I put them there." She said, "Thank you, Lord! You not only gave me the groceries, but you made the Devil pay for it."

I like to start with something funny. I heard about this Mother. One Sunday morning, she entered her son's bedroom and said, "Son, wake up. It's time to go to church." He groaned, rolled over, and said, "No, Mom, I'm not attending church today." She said, "What do you mean you're not going? Why not? He said, "Mom, I'll give you two good reasons. Number one, I don't like those people. And number two, they don't like me." She said, "Son, that's no excuse. I'll give you two Better reasons why you SHOULD, too. Number one, you're 59 years old, and number two, you're the Pastor."

I like to start with something funny. I heard about this middle-aged woman. She had a heart attack. On the operating table, she asked God, "If this was it?" God said, "No, you have 40 more years." Upon recovery, she decided to stay in the hospital. She would have a facelift, tummy tuck, and liposuction -- extreme makeover two months later, as she was leaving the hospital. A car hit and killed her. She got to heaven and said, "God, I thought you said I had 40 more years." God said, "I'm sorry. I didn't recognize you."

I like to start with something funny. I heard about these four Catholic ladies. They were bragging about their sons. The first one said, "My son is a Priest. Everyone calls him ' Father ' when he walks into the room." The second one said my son is a Bishop. Everyone calls him ' Your Grace ' when he walks into the room. The third one said my son is a Cardinal. Everyone calls him ' Your Eminence ' when he walks into the room. The fourth lady said, my son is 6 foot 3, has broad shoulders, is incredibly good-looking, and dresses impeccably well. When he enters the room, all the ladies say, "Oh, My God!"

I like to start with something funny. I heard about this lady. She was on the airplane reading her Bible. The man beside her said, "You don't believe all that stuff in there, do you?" She said, "Of course I do. It's the Bible." He said, "What about that guy that got swallowed by the whale?" She said, "You mean Jonah. Yes, I believe that too." He asked, "How could he live that long inside a fish?" She momentarily thought about it and said, "I don't know. When I get to heaven, I must ask him." He said sarcastically, "What if he is not in heaven?" She said, "Then you will have to ask him."

I like to start with something funny. I heard about this lady. She surprised a burglar in her kitchen late one night. She was home alone and didn't have any weapons. She didn't know what she would do. Finally, she thought, I would say a Scripture verse. She shouted, "Acts 2:38." The burglar suddenly froze in his tracks; he wouldn't move. Soon, the police arrived. They were amazed that a woman with no weapon could do this. They asked the burglar, "What about that Scripture that had such an effect on you?" He said, "Scripture. What scripture? She said she had an axe and two thirty-eights (.38s)."

I like to start with something funny. I heard about these two ladies who died and went to heaven. Peter met them at the gate, saying, "You will be happy here if you follow one main rule: don't step on a duck." If you step on a duck, they make a terrible racket. A week later, one of the ladies accidentally stepped on a duck. Peter came up to her with this highly unattractive man. Nothing appealing about him whatsoever. [Peter] Said, "As your punishment, I'll chain you to this man." Seeing this, the other lady was cautious. A month later, Peter approached her with this incredibly handsome man. He had a fantastic physique and looked like a movie star. He chained them together. The lady was thrilled. She told him, "I don't know what I did to get chained to you." He said, "I don't know what you did, ma'am, but I stepped on a duck."

I like to start with something funny. I heard about this lady. She saw this little older man sitting on his front porch in his rocking chair. He always seemed to be so happy. She finally approached him and said, "I can't help but notice. You're always smiling; you're always in a good mood. What is your secret for such a long, happy life?" He said, "That's easy. I smoke three packs of cigarettes every day. I eat nothing but junk food, and I never exercise. She said, "That's amazing! How old are you?" He said, "26."

I like to start with something funny. I heard about this Sunday morning church service. It was going just fine. All of a sudden, this lightning bolt hit. When the smoke cleared, Satan himself was standing behind the podium. People panicked and ran out of the building as fast as they could. Satan stood there with glee. But suddenly, his mood changed when he noticed a woman sitting in the front row just as calm as can be. He said, "Lady, do you know who I am?" She said, "I sure do." He said, "Aren't you afraid of me?" She said. "No, I'm not." He said, "Why not?" She said, "Why should I be … For 30 years, I have married your brother."

I like to start with something funny. I heard about this blonde lady. (And you may be married to a beautiful, bright, intelligent blonde). But this blonde was at Target and saw this thermos on the shelf. She asked the clerk what it was. He said, "That's a thermos. You've never used one of those?" She said, "No. What does it do?" He said, "It keeps things hot, and it keeps things cold." The next day, she showed up at work with it. Her boss said, "I've never seen You with a thermos. What do you have in there?" She said, "Two popsicles and some coffee."

I like to start with something funny. I heard about three people: a Russian, an American, and a blonde. They were talking one day. The Russian said, "Well, we were the first ones on the moon." The blonde said, "That's nothing. We're going to be the first ones on the sun." The Russians and the Americans laughed and said, "What are you talking about? You can't go to the sun. It's too hot. You'll burn up." The blonde said, "We're not that dumb; we're going to go at night."

Chapter 3

MARITAL JESTS
Laughing Through Love: Hilarious Tales and Quips from Married Life

I like to start with something funny. I heard about this lady who was shopping with her husband. He asked her not to buy any new clothes. Well, she saw this dress in the window and decided to try it on; she liked it so much she bought it in secret. A couple of days later, the husband discovered it. He was so upset. She explained to him that when she tried it on, it looked so good Satan tempted her to buy it, and she couldn't resist it. He said, "Why didn't you do what the Scriptures said and say, 'Get behind me Satan!'" She said, 'I did, and he told me it looked even better from a distance.'

I like to start with something funny. I heard about this wife. She was taking a nap on Valentine's Day during the afternoon. When she woke up, she called her husband and said, "Honey, I just had a dream that you brought me a beautiful diamond ring for Valentine's Day. What do you think this dream means?" He said, "You will find out tonight." That evening, he brought home a beautifully wrapped, small package. She opened it up so excited. It was a book entitled, "The Meaning of Dreams."

I like to start with something funny. I heard about this lady who died, and she found herself standing at the Pearly Gates. Saint Peter said, "You can't come in unless you correctly spell a word." She said, "What word?" He said, "Any word." So she spelled the word "L-O-V-E." Peter said, "Welcome to heaven." Then Peter asked her if she would take his place. He instructed her, "If anybody comes, just follow the same procedure." In a few minutes, the lady sees her ex-husband coming up. She said, "What are you doing here?" He said, "I just had a heart attack. Did I make it to heaven?" She said, "No, not yet. You have to spell a word correctly." He said, "What word?" After a long pause, she said, "Czechoslovakia."

I like to start with something funny. I heard about this husband. He was quietly reading his newspaper when his wife snuck up behind him and hit him in the head with a frying pan. He said, "What was that for?" She said, "That was for the piece of paper I found in your pocket with the name Mary Lou on it." He said, "Aw honey, that's just one of the horses I bet on at last week's racetrack." She apologized and went about her business. Two days later, she hit him on the head with a bigger frying pan. When he came to, he said, "What in the world was that for? She said, "Your horse just called."

I like to start with something funny. I heard about this husband who died. He left his wife $20,000. After the funeral, his wife told a friend that she was broke. The friend said, "What do you mean you're broke? I thought you said you had $20,000". She said, "Well, I spent $5,000 on the funeral and $15,000 on the Memorial Stone". The friend said, "Wow, that's some kind of stone. How big was it"? She held up her finger and said, "Three and a half karats."

I like to start with something funny. I heard about this groom. At the wedding rehearsal, he told the minister, "I'll make a deal with you. If, during the vows, you'll leave out all that love, honor, and obey stuff, I'll give you $100." He slipped a $100 bill into the minister's hand and walked

40

away with a smile. The next day during the ceremony, the minister asked him, "Do you promise to bow down before your wife, take her breakfast in bed, to fulfill her every desire?" He gulped in astonishment and said weakly, "I do." Then he whispered in the minister's ear, "I thought we had a deal." The minister handed him his money back and said, "Your wife made me a much better offer."

I like to start with something funny. I heard about this husband and wife. They were celebrating their 60th birthdays together. An angel suddenly appeared and said, "God was going to grant them each special request." They were so excited. The wife said, "I request that we would be able to travel all over the world." Poof, when the smoke cleared, "She had tickets in their hand." The husband hung his head in shame. He said, "I request that I will be married to a woman 30 years younger than me." Poof, when the smoke cleared, he was 90 years old.

I like to start with something funny. I heard about this elderly couple. The couple had been married for over 60 years. They were at a church fellowship, and someone asked them the secret of their success. The man said he always treated his wife respectfully and took her on trips worldwide. He said, "For our 25th wedding anniversary, I took her to Beijing, China." Everyone politely applauded, and then someone asked, "What did you do for your 50th wedding anniversary?" He said, "I went back and picked her up."

I like to start with something funny. I heard about this husband and wife. They had been arguing. Now, they were giving each other the silent treatment. The man had to get up early the next day and catch a flight. He needed his wife to wake him up. Not wanting to break the silence, he left a note on her bed that said, "Please wake me up at 5 AM." The next day, he woke at 8 o'clock and missed his flight. He was so upset and thought I would go and find out why she didn't wake me up. There was a note on his side of the bed; it said, "Wake up, it's 5."

I like to start with something funny. I heard about this man and his wife. They argued for months over who should make the coffee in the morning. The man thought it was the wife's job, and she disagreed. After several heated debates, she finally said, "I can prove from the Bible that it's your job." He said, "There's nothing in the Bible about making coffee." She said, "Sure, there is." She called him over, opened her Bible, and pointed to the book of "Hebrews."

I like to start with something funny. I heard about this country couple. The couple was celebrating their 50th wedding anniversary. They'd never argued before. Someone asked them the secret of their success. The husband explained that the wife's horse refused to go as they left the church for their honeymoon. She got off, looked at the horse in the eyes, and said, "That's one." He went a little bit further and stopped again. She got off, looked at the horse in the eyes, and said, "That's two." He went a little bit more, but once again, he stopped. This time, she got off, pulled out her revolver, and shot the horse dead. The husband said, "What in the world are you doing? You just can't shoot an animal." She looked at him and said, "That's one."

I like to start with something funny. I heard about this man. Somebody had stolen his wife's credit card. A few months later, the company called him and said, "Sir, we got good news; we found the credit card." The man said, "Tell the thief to keep it. He spends less than my wife."

I like to start with something funny. I heard about this guy. He was late to work for the third day in a row. His boss said sarcastically, "Okay, What's your excuse this time." He said, "I'm so sorry, but my wife asked to drive me to work. And I told her she didn't need to, but she insisted and said she could be ready in 10 minutes. But then, when we left, the drawbridge was up, and I had to swim across the river, fighting off alligators. Then a helicopter picked me up [and] put me on top of a building. I ran down 60 stairs and got here as quickly as possible." His boss shook his head and said, "You expect me to believe that? No woman can get dressed in just 10 minutes."

I like to start with something funny. I heard about this man who was very stingy with his money. Just before his death, he made his wife promise him that she would have him buried with the $50,000 he had saved. His wife reluctantly agreed. At the funeral, before they closed the casket, she snuck in this small wooden box. Her friend said, "Surely, you just didn't bury the money, did you?" The wife said, "Of course I did. I'm a Christian, I can't lie." She said, "You mean you just buried $50,000?" The wife said, "Yes, I did. I wrote a check."

Chapter 4

FAMILY WITTICISMS
Laughs and Love: Unforgettable Moments of Family Humor

I like to start with something funny. I heard about this old country farmer. He was taking his nephew camping for the first time. His nephew, who had five degrees, was one of the most intelligent men alive; they set their tent up and quickly fell asleep. In the middle of the night, the farmer woke his nephew up and said, 'Look up, what do you see?' He said, 'I see millions of stars.' The farmer said, 'I know that, but what does it tell you?' He said, 'Astronomically, it tells me billions of galaxies. Meteorologically, it tells me it's going to be a beautiful day. Theologically, it tells me God is a great Creator. What does it tell you? The old farmer shook his head and said, "Somebody stole our tent."

I like to start with something funny. I heard about this man. He was on vacation in Jerusalem with his family when his mother-in-law suddenly died. He went to plan to get her body back home. The consulate said, "It would cost $5,000 to have her shipped. But he could have her buried in Jerusalem for $150." The man thought about it a moment and said, "I'd like to have her body shipped home." The consulate said, "Wow, you must have loved your mother-in-law." The man said, "Naw, it's not so much that. I remember this case many years ago when they buried somebody, and on the third day, they arose. I can't take that chance."

I like to start with something funny. I heard about these three sons who left home and went out and prospered. They returned to talk about the gifts they brought their elderly mother. The first son said, "I built mom a big house." The second one said, "I got her a fancy car." The third son said, "Since mom loves to read the Bible, but she can barely see anymore, I got her a specially trained parrot that can quote the entire Bible." A few months later, they received a letter from their mother. It said, "Milton, the house you built me is too big. Gerald, the car you bought me is way too small. But, my dearest Donald, your simple gift is my favorite. The chicken is delicious."

I like to start with something funny. I heard about these two evil brothers. They were wealthy. They attended the same church and, on the surface, appeared to be good Christians. One of the brothers suddenly died. The remaining brother sought out the pastor and handed him a large donation. He said, I only have one condition. At the funeral, you must say my brother was a saint. The pastor agreed and deposited the check. At the funeral, the pastor said, "This man was evil. He lied, he stole, [and] he cheated people." After going on and on for several minutes, he finally said, "But compared to his brother, he was a saint."

Chapter 5

CHILDREN RIB-TICKLERS
Giggles Galore: Hilarious Tales of Kids' Comedy

I like to start with something funny. I heard about these two boys, ages 4 and 6; they were brothers. They were spending the night at their grandmother's house. She told them to make sure they said their prayers before they went to bed. They went into the bedroom and got on their knees. The youngest boy started praying at the top of his lungs, 'God, I pray for a new bicycle; I pray for a new PlayStation; I pray for a new DVD.' His brother punched him and said, 'Why are you screaming? God isn't deaf.' He said, "I know that, but grandmother is."

I like to start with something funny. I heard about this little girl. She was sitting on her grandfather's lap. She noticed how wrinkled his face was as she contemplated the difference between hers and his. She said, "Granddaddy, Did God make you?" He laughed and said, "Yes, honey, God made me long ago." Well, she said, "Did God make me?" He said, "Yes, God made you just a little while ago." She thought about it momentarily and said, "Granddaddy, God's getting better, isn't he?"

I like to start with something funny. I heard about a mother who invited some people for dinner. She turned to her five-year-old daughter at the table and asked, "Honey, would you like to say the blessings?" The little girl replied, "I don't what to say." The mom replied, "Just say what you hear mommy say." The little girl bowed and said, "Oh Lord, Why did I invite these people to dinner?"

I like to start with something funny. I heard about this little girl. She was attending a wedding for the first time. She asked her mom, "Why is the bride wearing all white?" The mom smiled and said, "Oh, white is the color of happiness. Today is the happiest day of her life." The little girl thought, "Why is the groom wearing all black?"

I like to start with something funny. I heard about this little boy. He was out in his front yard playing. This man came walking down the street, frustrated. He said, "Son, I'm lost. Can you tell me how to get to the post office?" The little boy said, "Yeah, go to the stop sign and turn left; it's right around the corner." He thanked him. He said, "By the way, I'm the new pastor here in town. If you'd come to my church this Sunday, I'll tell you how to get to heaven." The little boy said, "No thanks. You don't even know how to get to the post office."

I like to start with something funny. I heard about this little girl. She asked her mother how the human race got started. The mother explained how God made Adam and Eve; they had children, and on and on, and here we are today. A few days later, she asked her father the same question. He explained how many years ago there were monkeys. Little by little, they became more like people, and now here we are. Confused, she returned to her mom and said, "Mom, you said God created people. Dad said we came from monkeys. How can that be?" She said, "Oh honey, that's easy. I told you about my side of the family. Dad told you about his.

I like to start with something funny. I heard about this little 3-year-old boy. He had a sore throat. His mom took him to the doctor, and the doctor put his stethoscope on his chest to listen to his lungs, and he said to the little boy, "Okay, just be still, buddy. I will check to see if Barney's in here." The little boy said, "Jesus is in my heart, but Barney's in my underwear."

PART II

NON-SPIRITUAL HUMOR
Everyday Laughter: A Collection of Lighthearted Moments

Chapter 6

ANIMAL BITS
Wild and Whimsical: Laugh-Out-Loud Animal Antics

I like to start with something funny. I heard about this cat and mouse. The animals died on the same day and went to heaven. After a few weeks, Peter asked the mouse, "How did he like it so far?" He said, "Ah Peter, it's great ... But it's so big. Do you think I can get some roller skates?" Peter said, "No problem. I got the mouse some roller skates." A few weeks later, he saw the cat and asked, "How did he like it?" He said, "Ah, Peter, I love it. And just when I thought it couldn't get any better, I discovered the Meals on Wheels."

I like to start with something funny. I heard about a man whom a bear was chasing. The bear cornered the man, and the man prayed, 'Dear God, please make this bear a Christian bear.' So, God did as he said. And the bear said, 'Dear God, please bless this food I'm about to eat.'

I like to start with something funny. I heard about this minister who was out bear hunting. He searched through the woods but saw no sign of a bear. Finally, in frustration, he threw his gun down and went down to the stream to cool off. About that time, he saw this giant grizzly bear racing toward him. He knelt and said, "Please, God protect me. I'm asking God to convert this bear into a Christian." Miraculously, the bear froze, put up both paws toward the heavens, and said, "Thank You, Lord, for this food I'm about to eat."

I like to start with something funny. I heard about this blond lady. She was working with the weed eater in the yard when she accidentally cut off her cat's tail. He was in the bushes, and she didn't see him. She felt so bad. She grabbed the cat, grabbed the tail, and told her friend she was going to Walmart. She said, "Walmart? Why Walmart?" She said, "Hello. They're the largest 'Retailer' in the world."

I like to start with something funny. According to the Alaskan Department of Fish and Game. While male and female reindeer grow antlers in the summer, male reindeer lose their antlers in early November at the start of winter. Female reindeer keep theirs until the spring. This logic means that all of Santa's reindeer, from Rudolph to Blixen, had to be female. We should have known only women could drag around a fat man, wearing a red velvet suit all around the world in one night, and not get lost.

I like to start with something funny. I heard about this blond lady. She was trying to get to sleep one night. But her next-door neighbor's dogs were barking so loud, she couldn't. She finally had had enough. She got up and told her husband she would do something about it. She returned a few minutes later, and the dogs were barking louder than ever. He said, "What did you do?" She said, "I put the dogs in our backyard. Let's see how they like it."

I like to start with something funny. I heard about this burglar who broke into a home one night. While stealing the stereo, he heard a voice saying, "Jesus is watching you." He froze in his tracks and shined the flashlight around the room. And he saw a parrot over in the corner. He said, "Did you say that to me?" The parrot said, "Yes, I'm just trying to warn you." He said, "Warn me, what are you talking about? Who are you?" The parrot said, "My name is Moses." The burglar laughed and said, "What kind of crazy people would name a parrot Moses?" The parrot said, "The same kind of people that would name a 150-pound Rottweiler Jesus."

I like to start with something funny. I heard about this man. He was walking up to a country store. A little boy was sitting on the front porch with a large dog sitting next to him. The man said, "Son, does your dog bite?" He said, "No sir, my dog doesn't bite." The man reached down to pet the dog, and the dog took about half his arm off. He pulled it back and said, "Son, I thought you said your dog didn't bite." The little boy said, "That's not my dog."

Chapter 7

SPORTS ANTICS
Playful Pursuits: Unforgettable Athletic Adventures

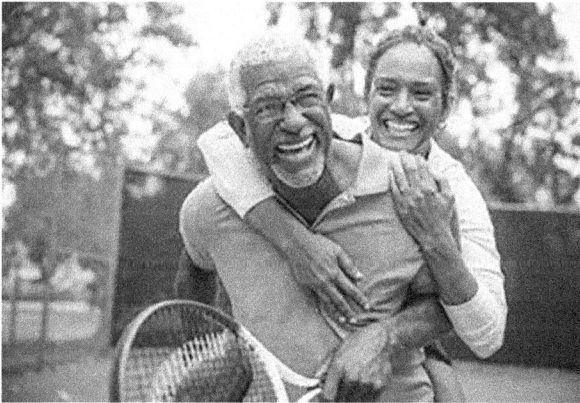

I like to start with something funny. I heard about these two professional baseball players. They were discussing whether or not there would be baseball up in heaven. They made an agreement that whoever died first would come back and tell the other one if, indeed, there was baseball in heaven. A few months later, one of the men died. Just like he promised, he came back. He said to his friend, "I got good news, and I got terrible news. The good news is baseball is up in heaven; the bad news is God has scheduled you to pitch next Thursday."

I like to start with something funny. I heard about this professor. He was going to prove to his students that there is no God. He said, "God, if you're real, knock me off this platform. I'm giving you 15 minutes to do it." With every minute, he taunted God, "God, I'm still waiting. I'm still here." At the last minute, [a] 300-pound football player walking down the hallway overheard what he was saying. He took off running toward him full blast, put his shoulders down, and sent him flying off the platform. The professor stood in a daze and asked, "What did you do that for?" [The] Football player replied, "God said He was busy, so he sent me."

Chapter 8

OCCUPATIONAL LAUGHS
Workplace Wit: Hilarious Tales from the Job

I like to start with something funny. I heard about this blond lady. She was driving down the freeway when she got pulled over by a female police officer, who also happened to be blond. The officer asked for a driver's license. She dug in her purse, getting increasingly agitated, and couldn't find it. Finally, [she] asked the officer, 'What does it look like?' She said, 'It's a little square with your picture.' The lady found her mirror, saw herself, said 'Oh' and handed it to the officer. The officer looked in the mirror and saw herself, handed it back, and said, 'You can go. I didn't realize you were a police officer."

I like to start with something funny. I heard about these new police recruits. The officer was taking his final exam. He was in front of a large classroom. The sergeant asked him, "What would you do if you had to arrest your mother-in-law?" Without missing a beat, he said, "Call for backup."

I like to start with something funny. I heard about this man who lived in the country. One night, he heard some noise and saw burglars stealing things from his barn. He ran to the phone and dialed 9-1-1. But the dispatcher said, "I'm sorry, sir. There are no patrol cars available. You need to lock your doors, and we will get somebody there as soon as possible." He hung up, so frustrated. After about 30 seconds, he called back and said, "Mam, don't worry about it, you don't need to send anybody. I shot all the burglars." Ninety seconds later … three patrol cars, one sheriff, and two ambulances showed up, and they caught the burglars red-handed. The sheriff went over afterward and said, "I thought you said you shot the burglars." The man said, "I thought you said nobody was available."

I like to start with something funny. I heard about this kindergarten teacher. She was walking around her classroom as her students drew pictures. She noticed this one little girl drawing so intently. She asked her, 'What was she drawing?' The little girl said, 'She was drawing a picture of God.' The teacher laughed. She said, 'Aw honey, nobody knows what God looks like." Without missing a beat, the little girl said, 'They will in a minute.'

I like to start with something funny. I heard about this kindergarten teacher. She was teaching her students about self-esteem. She told the class, "Anyone that felt dumb, she asked them to stand up." She didn't think anybody would stand. She'll make the point that no one is dumb. About that time, little Johnny stood up. She thought, "Oh no, now what will I do?" She said, "Now, Johnny, Do you feel dumb?" He said, "No, ma'am, I just hate seeing you standing there alone."

I like to start with something funny. I heard about this airplane that was about to crash. There were four passengers but only three parachutes. The first passenger said, 'I'm a leading heart surgeon; my patients need me.

He grabbed the first parachute and jumped.' The second passenger said, 'I'm a rocket scientist, one of the smartest men in the world; my country needs me. He took the second parachute and jumped. The third passenger was Pope John Paul. He told the fourth passenger, a 10-year-old boy scout, 'Son, I'm old and frail. You take the last parachute.' The Boy Scout said, 'That's okay, sir, there's still two parachutes left. The world's smartest man just jumped out with my backpack."

I like to start with something funny. I heard about this scientist. He said to God, "We decided we no longer need you." We can clone people -- transplant, harvest, and do all kinds of things once considered miraculous. I said that's fine. Let's have a man-making contest to prove you don't need me. The only requirement is that you have to make man out of dirt. The scientist said, "Great." He reached down quickly for a hand full of dirt. God said, "Not so quick. Go get your dirt."

I like to start with something funny. I heard about this archeologist in New York. He dug down 10 feet and found traces of copper wiring dating back 100 years. He concluded that New Yorkers had a telephone network over 100 years ago. Not to be outdone, an archeologist from California dug down 20 feet and found copper wiring dating back 200 years. He concluded that Californians had massive communications networks 100 years earlier than New Yorkers. Upon hearing this, Bubba from Texas dug down 30 feet on his farm and found absolutely nothing. He concluded that 300 years ago, Texans had already gone wireless.

I like to start with something funny. I heard about this airplane; it was about to land. The flight attendant approached the loudspeaker and said, "We'd like you to help welcome our new copilot. He's about to make his first commercial landing. So, give him a big applause when the plane stops." A few minutes later, the plane made an extremely bumpy landing -- bouncing up and down. She came back on and said, "Thanks for flying with us today. Don't forget to tell our new copilot which one of his three landings you liked best."

I like to start with something funny. I heard about this reporter. He was visiting churches all across the country. While in New York, he noticed this golden telephone on the wall and a sign that said, "Calls, 10 thousand dollars per minute." He asked the pastor what it meant. The pastor explained, "That was a direct line to heaven. If you were willing to pay the price, you could talk directly to God." He continued to visit different churches and saw the same phone with the same sign. When he finally made it to Texas, he saw the phone. But the sign said, "Calls, 25 cents per minute." Intrigued, he asked the pastor, "Why it was so much cheaper?" The pastor said, "You're in Texas. Now, it's a local call."

CONCLUSION

Take Charge of Your Joy

Casey, let's take more time to review our discussion and conclude. People can experience sadness, the blues, or a lack of self-esteem. Often, individuals live in stress and tension, prioritizing work over leisure. As stated in Ecclesiastes 3:4, there are times for weeping, laughing, mourning, and dancing. We fill our lives with emotional seasons that may include moments of joy and sorrow intertwining. We delivered short, clean, tested jokes to maintain hope, better prepare for these seasons, and serve our audience. These anecdotes, which exude a feel-good factor, are just to make us laugh, whether you read them for yourself or tell them to your listeners. Joy, joy, joy! There are over 100 tested, short, clean jokes in this unprecedented compilation that remind us to be joyful and encourage laughter. They will hit the spot, and your audience and you will be satisfied. "A joyful heart is a good medicine, but a crushed spirit dries up the bones" (Pr. 17:22).

God wants you to find joy in Him daily, not other people and situations. So, you can rejoice in your excellent relationship with Him because Jesus Christ has made you a friend of God. Likewise, we conceptualized the sequential process of telling a funny joke: framing, telling, and responding -- The Humor Exchange -- to help people come to faith in Jesus when they read or say a joke. In many ways, the method is similar to attending church and giving a speech.

Similarly, framing sets the audience's expectations for opening a speech or invitation to church. Telling is like the body of a speech or the friend who attends church, which is the pivot. And as the pastor closes a speech by inviting people to accept Christ, responding to a joke is similar to laughing at a joke. So, are you ready for it? You cannot depend on someone else to make you joyful. God has given you the ability to take responsibility for your joy and be beside yourself with happiness. Casey, is there enough support for this route? Are there any additional resources you need? Do you have any options for rearranging your choices? When can you start acting?

Therefore, you will know the critical point's summary – from framing to telling to responding. It emphasizes the idea of a reciprocal exchange of laughter and pleasure between the joke teller and their audience. So, you'll bring joy and encourage laughter. And you'll rise to the top with 100 short, clean jokes! Hopefully, you'll share your takeaways and memories with your friends. Tell everything you remember about this book over and over. That is a little bit here and there. Therefore, I will outline these earlier lessons below. I hope I wrote into enough space. You'll understand the lessons the same way I do if you follow these steps:

This book is fun and a delightful blend of spiritual joys and non-spiritual humor, divided into two distinct parts. The first part explores various aspects of everyday life, with chapters dedicated to male wisecracks, female quips, marital jests, family witticisms, and children rib-ticklers. Readers will enjoy the lighthearted and relatable humor offered in these chapters. I provide a diverse range of humorous content in the book's second part, which focuses on different sources of laughter. This section includes chapters on animal bits, sports antics, and occupational laughs. Readers can escape into laughter with these amusing anecdotes and situations about animals, sports, and different professions. This book provides readers insightful, uplifting moments and lighthearted, entertaining laughs, balancing spiritual joy and non-spiritual humor.

By taking charge of your joy, you elevate others' self-worth and help them feel like they have something to offer. You serve your audience with a sense of humor and make them feel good about themselves. When you embrace happiness, you also become a lifter. You make your listeners feel better about themselves. You speak positively of others. You lift with words, hugs, love, and value they give you – testable, short, clean jokes. You make your audience feel important. Through your genuine passion and care, Jesus demonstrates His love. Your audience feels better about themselves, finds the good, and becomes an encouragement to you when you lift them. Continue to see people through His eyes - change how you speak, treat, and respond to them. The Lord designed you. He does not make mistakes. You love them because The Father loves you. He has a plan for their lives, and you want to be part of it. Choose to see the good. Look for the right; focus on success. Don't just see the good; say the good. With these anecdotes, you'll inspire others. Don't fake joy or manufacture happiness; count it all as joy.

Keep your expectations high. People tend to become what they think we expect them to become. You can set them up for success or failure by your expectations. People tend to become what they believe we expect them to be. Excessive criticism can tear down and demoralize a team if you expect them to be lazy, uncreative, negative, and "dead wood" performers. Contrastingly, treating people like "stars" or winners makes them more likely to succeed. Educators teach children to become what we tell them they are; psychologists call this the Pygmalion effect (e.g., the best leaders expect followers, the best teachers expect students to learn, etc.). Please encourage them to be their best by treating them as they could be. There is a possibility.

Lift and encourage with powerful words: I love you, I believe in you, I believe in your potential. God will use you, for sure. I am thankful for you! Keep saying the right things at the right time. Be a lifter. When you bless others, they'll bless you as well. You matter to me! I thank God for you!

Replace wrong thinking with the truth of His Word. The value of something is how much someone is willing to pay for it. He gave a high price for our sins (1Pe. 1:18-19). His blood redeemed us. He determined our worth on the Cross. Your joy rubs off on others when it is evident and displayed; your laughter, smile, and joy make others feel good. Your happiness brings joy and comfort to those who receive it. The expression of joy can help change circumstances and the lives of others now instead of regretting not reaching them earlier. Share your joy!

ACKNOWLEDGMENTS

Casey, As you reach the end of this book, you have my deepest gratitude for the time you've spent delving into these pages.

Many people helped me prepare this text. I give honor to whom honor is due. First and foremost, I always thank almighty God! He enabled me with faithfulness, gifts, and favor. May I always have an intense longing to bring glory to His Kingdom, equip disciples to do His work, and build up the church.

I'm grateful for family and friends who prayed and supported me in writing this book. I penned this book not with pen and ink but with the Spirit of the living God. I pray I've carved these words and planted the seed in your heart. I planted the seed in your hearts, but it was God who made it grow. And they're good, helpful, and encouraging; others and you will water it. And God makes the seed grow, and this word continues to work in you who believe." I hope these multiplied blessings touch your soul, and you'll fan the flames to those who have eyes but refuse to see and ears but refuse to hear.

Father, I try to find common ground with everyone, doing everything possible to save some. Make your face shine upon me so I reach the most significant number of new and growing believers to draw nearer to You!

Proclaiming the Greatness of God:
A Joyful Expression of Faith

Now Jericho was shut up inside and outside because of the people of Israel. None went out, and none came in. ² And the Lord said to Joshua, "See, I have given Jericho into your hand, with its king and mighty men of valor. ³ You shall march around the city, all the men of war going around the city once. Thus, shall you do for six days. ⁴ Seven priests shall bear seven trumpets of rams' horns before the ark. On the seventh day you shall march around the city seven times, and the priests shall blow the trumpets. ⁵ And when they make a long blast with the ram's horn, when you hear the sound of the trumpet, then all the people shall shout with a great shout, and the wall of the city will fall down flat,[a] and the people shall go up, everyone straight before him." ⁶ So Joshua the son of Nun called the priests and said to them, "Take up the ark of the covenant and let seven priests bear seven trumpets of rams' horns before the ark of the Lord." ⁷ And he said to the people, "Go forward. March around the city and let the armed men pass on before the ark of the Lord."

⁸ And just as Joshua had commanded the people, the seven priests bearing the seven trumpets of rams' horns before the Lord went forward, blowing the trumpets, with the ark of the covenant of the Lord following them. ⁹ The armed men were walking before the priests who were blowing the trumpets, and the rear guard was walking after the ark, while the trumpets blew continually. ¹⁰ But Joshua commanded the people, "You shall not shout or make your voice heard, neither shall any word go out of

your mouth, until the day I tell you to shout. Then you shall shout." [11] So he caused the ark of the Lord to circle the city, going about it once. And they came into the camp and spent the night in the camp.

[12] Then Joshua rose early in the morning, and the priests took up the ark of the Lord. [13] And the seven priests bearing the seven trumpets of rams' horns before the ark of the Lord walked on, and they blew the trumpets continually. And the armed men were walking before them, and the rear guard was walking after the ark of the Lord, while the trumpets blew continually. [14] And the second day they marched around the city once and returned into the camp. So, they did for six days.

[15] On the seventh day they rose early, at the dawn of day, and marched around the city in the same manner seven times. It was only on that day that they marched around the city seven times. [16] And at the seventh time, when the priests had blown the trumpets, Joshua said to the people, "Shout, for the Lord has given you the city. [17] And the city and all that is within it shall be devoted to the Lord for destruction.[b] Only Rahab the prostitute and all who are with her in her house shall live, because she hid the messengers whom we sent. [18] But you, keep yourselves from the things devoted to destruction, lest when you have devoted them, you take any of the devoted things and make the camp of Israel a thing for destruction and bring trouble upon it. [19] But all silver and gold, and every vessel of bronze and iron, are holy to the Lord; they shall go into the treasury of the Lord." [20] So the people shouted, and the trumpets were blown. As soon as the people heard the sound of the trumpet, the people shouted a great shout, and the wall fell down flat, so that the people went up into the city, every man straight before him, and they captured the city.
(Js. 6:1-20)

The Lord said to Gideon, "The people with you are too many for me to give the Midianites into their hand, lest Israel boast over me, saying, 'My own hand has saved me.'
(Jg. 7:2)

And he said to them, "Look at me, and do likewise. When I come to the outskirts of the camp, do as I do.
(Jg. 7:17)

And the men of Israel and Judah rose with a shout and pursued the Philistines as far as Gath and the gates of Ekron, so that the wounded Philistines fell on the way from Shaaraim as far as Gath and Ekron. (1Sa. 17:52)

Shout before the victory in anticipation. Shout after the victory in celebration.

Shout because God is faithful

Shout for joy in the Lord, O you righteous!
    Praise befits the upright.
2 Give thanks to the Lord with the lyre;
    make melody to him with the harp of ten strings!
3 Sing to him a new song;
    play skillfully on the strings, with loud shouts.
4 For the word of the Lord is upright,
    and all his work is done in faithfulness.
(Ps. 33:1-4)

Shout because God's protects me

The Lord is my light and my salvation;
    whom shall I fear?
The Lord is the stronghold[a] of my life;
    of whom shall I be afraid?
2 When evildoers assail me
    to eat up my flesh,
my adversaries and foes,
    it is they who stumble and fall.
3 Though an army encamp against me,
    my heart shall not fear;
though war arise against me,
    yet[b] I will be confident.
4 One thing have I asked of the Lord,
    that will I seek after:

that I may dwell in the house of the Lord
   all the days of my life,
to gaze upon the beauty of the Lord
   and to inquire[c] in his temple.
5 For he will hide me in his shelter
   in the day of trouble;
he will conceal me under the cover of his tent;
   he will lift me high upon a rock.
6 And now my head shall be lifted up
   above my enemies all around me,
and I will offer in his tent
   sacrifices with shouts of joy;
I will sing and make melody to the Lord.
(Ps. 27:1-6)

Shout because God is great

Make a joyful noise to the Lord, all the earth!
  2 Serve the Lord with gladness!
Come into his presence with singing!
  3 Know that the Lord, he is God!
It is he who made us, and we are his;[a]
   we are his people, and the sheep of his pasture.
(Ps. 100:1-3)

Clap your hands, all peoples!

   Shout to God with loud songs of joy!
2 For the Lord, the Most High, is to be feared,
   a great king over all the earth.
(Ps. 47:1-2)

Shout because God answers prayer.

May we shout for joy over your salvation,
   and in the name of our God set up our banners!
May the Lord fulfill all your petitions!

⁶ Now I know that the Lord saves his anointed;
   he will answer him from his holy heaven
   with the saving might of his right hand.
⁷ Some trust in chariots and some in horses,
   but we trust in the name of the Lord our God.
(Ps. 20:5-7)

Shout because Jesus is alive, and Jesus is here.

Most of the crowd spread their cloaks on the road, and others cut branches from the trees and spread them on the road. ⁹ And the crowds that went before him and that followed him were shouting, "Hosanna to the Son of David! Blessed is he who comes in the name of the Lord! Hosanna in the highest!"
(Mt. 21:8-9)

Shout because it's what I am going to do in heaven!

After this I heard what seemed to be the loud voice of a great multitude in heaven, crying out,

"Hallelujah!
(Re. 19:1)

- First North Little Rock Assembly of God Church

APPENDIX B

Joyful Scriptures:
Finding Laughter and Humor in the Bible

A joyful heart is good medicine, but a crushed spirit dries up the bones (Pr. 17:22).

Then our mouth was filled with laughter, and our tongue with shouts of joy; then they said among the nations, "The Lord has done great things for them" (Ps. 126:2).

He will yet fill your mouth with laughter, and your lips with shouting (Jb. 8:21).

A time to weep, and a time to laugh; a time to mourn, and a time to dance (Ec. 3:4).

A glad heart makes a cheerful face, but by sorrow of heart the spirit is crushed (Pr. 15:13).

He who sits in the heavens laughs; the Lord holds them in derision (Ps. 2:4).

And Sarah said, "God has made laughter for me; everyone who hears will laugh over me" (Ge. 21:6).

Be glad in the Lord, and rejoice, O righteous, and shout for joy, all you upright in heart (Ps. 32:11)!

Let there be no filthiness nor foolish talk nor crude joking, which are out of place, but instead let there be thanksgiving (Ep. 5:4).

Even in laughter the heart may ache, and the end of joy may be grief (Pr. 14:13).

You make known to me the path of life; in your presence there is fullness of joy; at your right hand are pleasures forevermore

(Ps. 16:11).

I have set the Lord always before me; because he is at my right hand, I shall not be shaken. Therefore, my heart is glad, and my whole being rejoices; my flesh also dwells secure. For you will not abandon my soul to Sheol or let your holy one see corruption. You make known to me the path of life; in your presence there is fullness of joy; at your right hand are pleasures forevermore
(Ps. 16:8-11).

You have put more joy in my heart than they have when their grain and wine abound (Ps. 4:7).

But the Lord laughs at the wicked, for he sees that his day is coming (Ps. 37:13).

Rejoice in the Lord always; again, I will say, Rejoice (Ph. 4:4).

The Lord your God is in your midst, a mighty one who will save; he will rejoice over you with gladness; he will quiet you by his love; he will exult over you with loud singing (Zp. 3:17).

Let your speech always be gracious, seasoned with salt, so that you may know how you ought to answer each person (Cl. 4:6).

Yet I will rejoice in the Lord; I will take joy in the God of my salvation (Hb. 3:18).

Then I will go to the altar of God, to God my exceeding joy, and I will praise you with the lyre, O God, my God (Ps. 43:4).

For God gave us a spirit not of fear but of power and love and self-control. Therefore do not be ashamed of the testimony about our Lord, nor of me his prisoner, but share in suffering for the gospel by the power of God, who saved us and called us to a holy calling, not because of our works but because of his own purpose and grace, which he gave us in Christ Jesus before the ages began, and which now has been manifested through the appearing of our Savior Christ Jesus, who abolished death and brought life and immortality to light through the gospel (2Ti. 1:7-10).

Blessed is the man who walks not in the counsel of the wicked, nor stands in the way of sinners, nor sits in the seat of scoffers; but his delight is in the law of the Lord, and on his law, he meditates day and night. He is like a tree planted by streams of water that yields its fruit in its season, and its leaf does not wither. In all that he does, he prospers. The wicked are not so but are like chaff that the wind drives away. Therefore, the wicked will not stand in the judgment, nor sinners in the congregation of the righteous (Ps. 1:1-6).

Then Abraham fell on his face and laughed and said to himself, "Shall a child be born to a man who is a hundred years old? Shall Sarah, who is ninety years old, bear a child" (Ge. 17:17)?

Rejoice with those who rejoice, weep with those who weep (Ro. 12:15).

Strength and dignity are her clothing, and she laughs at the time to come (Pr. 31:25).

Is anyone among you suffering? Let him pray. Is anyone cheerful? Let him sing praise (Ja. 5:13).

"Blessed are you who are hungry now, for you shall be satisfied. "Blessed are you who weep now, for you shall laugh (Lk. 6:21).

To the choirmaster. A Psalm of the Sons of Korah. Clap your hands, all peoples! Shout to God with loud songs of joy (Ps. 47:1)!

Sorrow is better than laughter, for by sadness of face the heart is made glad (Ec. 7:3).

Whoever gives thought to the word will discover good, and blessed is he who trusts in the Lord (Pr. 16:20).

But God chose what is foolish in the world to shame the wise; God chose what is weak in the world to shame the strong; God chose what is low and despised in the world, even things that are not, to bring to nothing things that are, so that no human being might boast in the presence of God (1Co. 1:27-29).

If a wise man has an argument with a fool, the fool only rages and laughs, and there is no quiet (Pr. 29:9).

Let love be genuine. Abhor what is evil; hold fast to what is good (Ro. 12:9).

And at noon Elijah mocked them, saying, "Cry aloud, for he is a god. Either he is musing, or he is relieving himself, or he is on a journey, or perhaps he is asleep and must be awakened"
(1Ki. 18:27).

The natural person does not accept the things of the Spirit of God, for they are folly to him, and he is not able to understand them because they are spiritually discerned. The spiritual person judges all things but is himself to be judged by no one (1Co. 2:14-15).

"To what then shall I compare the people of this generation, and what are they like? They are like children sitting in the marketplace and calling to one another, "'we played the flute for you, and you did not dance; we sang a dirge, and you did not weep.' For John the Baptist has come eating no bread and drinking no wine, and you say, 'He has a demon.' The Son of Man has come eating and drinking, and you say, 'Look at him! A glutton and a drunkard, a friend of tax collectors and sinners' (Lk. 7:31-34)!

You keep him in perfect peace whose mind is stayed on you, because he trusts in you (Is. 26:3).

The good person out of the good treasure of his heart produces good, and the evil person out of his evil treasure produces evil, for out of the abundance of the heart his mouth speaks (Lk. 6:45).

I am a laughingstock to my friends; I, who called to God, and he answered me, a just and blameless man, am a laughingstock (Jb. 12:4).

Then the Lord opened the mouth of the donkey, and she said to Balaam, "What have I done to you, that you have struck me these three times?" And Balaam said to the donkey, "Because you have made a fool of me. I wish I had a sword in my hand, for then I would kill you." And the donkey said to Balaam, "Am I not your donkey, on which you have ridden all your life long to this day? Is it my habit to treat you this way?" And he said, "No" (Nu. 22:28-30).

The heart of the wise is in the house of mourning, but the heart of fools is in the house of mirth (Ec. 7:4).

Like a madman who throws firebrands, arrows, and death is the man who deceives his neighbor and says, "I am only joking" (Pr. 26:18-19).

The heart of the righteous ponders how to answer, but the mouth of the wicked pours out evil things (Pr. 15:28).

Then he said to them, "Go your way. Eat the fat and drink sweet wine and send portions to anyone who has nothing ready, for this day is holy to our Lord. And do not be grieved, for the joy of the Lord is your strength" (Ne. 8:10).

Be wretched and mourn and weep. Let your laughter be turned to mourning and your joy to gloom (Ja. 4:9).

On a Sabbath, while he was going through the grain fields, his disciples plucked and ate some heads of grain, rubbing them in their hands. But some of the Pharisees said, "Why are you doing what is not lawful to do on the Sabbath?" And Jesus answered them, "Have you not read what David did when he was hungry, he and those who were with him: how he entered the house of God and took and ate the bread of the Presence, which is not lawful for any but the priests to eat, and also gave it to those with him?" And he said to them, "The Son of Man is lord of the Sabbath"... (Lk. 6:1-21).

The vision of Isaiah the son of Amoz, which he saw concerning Judah and Jerusalem in the days of Uzziah, Jotham, Ahaz, and Hezekiah, kings of Judah. Hear, O heavens, and give ear, O earth; for the Lord has spoken: "Children have I reared and brought up, but they have rebelled against me. The ox knows its owner, and the donkey its master's crib, but Israel does not know, my people do not understand." Ah, sinful nation, a people laden with iniquity, offspring of evildoers, children who deal corruptly! They have forsaken the Lord, they have despised the Holy One of Israel, they are utterly estranged. Why will you still be struck down? Why will you continue to rebel? The whole head is sick, and the whole heart faint ... (Is.1:1-31).

Now the young man Samuel was ministering to the Lord under Eli. And the word of the Lord was rare in those days; there was no frequent vision (1Sa. 3:1).

But, as it is written, "What no eye has seen, nor ear heard, nor the heart of man imagined, what God has prepared for those who love him"— (1Co. 2:9).

For as the crackling of thorns under a pot, so is the laughter of the fools; this also is vanity (Ec. 7:6).

APPENDIX C

Memorable Milestones:
Celebrating Life's Blissful Moments

- Birth of a child (12.3%)

- Wedding day (11.5%)

- Birth of grandchildren (10%)

- Birth of another child (8.5%)

- Day of Retirement (7.4%)

- Moving into a new home (6.6%)

- Seeing children's first step (5.5%)

- Hearing child's first words (5.4%)

- Meeting person of your dreams (4.5%)

- First kiss with person you love (4.4%)

Festive Fun: Memorable Holiday One-Liners to Lighten the Mood

These holiday-themed one-liners are meant to be light-hearted and bring a smile to your face and laughter to your day during the public holidays or celebrations.

My wife and I also share good clean humor on "Witty Wednesday," approaching these jokes with sensitivity, appreciation, and respect. I hope they bring you some added light-heartedness to the holiday or occasion.

New Year's Day

Why did the scarecrow win an award on New Year's Day?
Because he was outstanding in his field all year round!

What do you call a snowman with a six-pack on New Year's Day?
An abdominal snowman!

Why did the calendar go to therapy on New Year's Day?
Because it had too many dates!

How do you catch a squirrel on New Year's Day?
Climb a tree and act like a nut!

What did one New Year's resolution say to the other?
"I'm committed to making this year a real challenge!"

Martin Luther King Jr. Day

Why did Martin Luther King Jr. go to art class?
Because he had a dream and he wanted to paint it!

What did Martin Luther King Jr. say to his computer?
"I have a keyboard!"

Why did Martin Luther King Jr. become a baker?
Because he wanted to make a world where everyone could have their cake and eat it too!

What did the traffic light say to Martin Luther King Jr.?
"Don't worry, I'll change so you can keep moving forward!"

Why did Martin Luther King Jr. always carry an umbrella?
Because he wanted to be prepared for any storm of injustice that might come his way!

Valentine's Day

What did the tortoise say on Valentine's Day?
I turt-ally love you.

What do you give your Valentine in France?
A big quiche.

What did the stamp say to the envelope on Valentine's Day?
I'm stuck on you!

How did the squirrel get his Valentine's attention?
He acted like a nut.

How do you keep a jewelry store safe on Valentine's Day?
You locket.

Why should you date a goalie?
He's a keeper.

What did the painter tell his girlfriend?
I love you with all my art.

What did the man with the broken leg tell his Valentine?
I have a crutch on you.

What's Cupid's favorite band?
Kiss!

Why did the sheriff lock up their valentine?
She stole their heart.

Why did the husband get his wife a kitten for Valentine's Day?
He thought it was the purr-fect present.

Anniversary

How do you remember your wedding anniversary?
Forget it once.

I bought my girlfriend a fridge for our anniversary.
I know it wasn't a great gift, but I loved seeing her face light up when she opened it.

I asked my wife if she'd like a new Diamond Ring to celebrate our anniversary.
She replied, "Nothing would make me happier!"

So, I got her nothing.
Our anniversary is coming up, so my wife told me that she would be happy as long as I get her something with a lot of diamonds in it. She's going to love this pack of playing cards.

My wife asked for something shiny that goes from 0 – 200 in five seconds or less for our anniversary.
I bought her a scale.
We're still not speaking.

I bought my wife a stripper pole for our anniversary and installed it in our bedroom. Whenever I ask her if she likes it, she just dances around the subject.

Marriage

A wife is shouting at her husband about not helping her with chores.
I'm cooking, cleaning, doing laundry, while you are sitting all day, waiting for me to bring you a beer.
What kind of a husband are you?
A patient one.

Adam spoke to God in the Garden of Eden. "I am lonely," said Adam. "I need someone around for company." "Very well," said God. "I will create a companion for you. One who will obey your every word, do all your chores along with cooking and cleaning for you." "Wonderful!" said Adam. "What will it take?" "For you, it will cost an arm and a leg," said God. "That seems pretty steep," said Adam. "What could I get for just a rib?"

My wife of 10 years left me because I didn't do enough chores.
It was devastating. I didn't do much to deserve it.

My husband is so cheap that when he dies, he's going to walk toward the light and turn it off.

Washington's Birthday

Why did George Washington chop down the cherry tree?
Because he couldn't tell a lie, but he sure could swing an axe!

How did George Washington sleep during the Revolutionary War?
He couldn't lie in bed, so he slept standing up!

Why did George Washington have trouble sleeping?
Because he couldn't get his mind off the country's debt!

What did George Washington say to his troops at Valley Forge?
"Sorry for the cold reception, but let's keep our spirits high!"

Why was George Washington a great gardener?
Because he always knew how to "plant" the seeds of success!

Spring

Which month of the year is the shortest?
May --it only has three letters.

Did you hear about the pregnant bedbug?
She's having her babies in the spring.

What emotion does a tree feel every Spring?
Relief!

Why are waterbeds so bouncy?
They're filled with spring water!

Why do bees have sticky hair in the Spring?
Because they use honeycombs!

What's the best time to go to the dentist in the Spring?
Tooth-hurty! (Two-thirty)

Why did the gardener bring a ladder in Spring?
To reach the high branches of the spring blossoms!

How do you fix a broken tomato plant in the Spring?
With tomato paste!

Why did the tree go to the dentist in Spring?
To get a root canal!

Vacation

Is Sand Hot?
Of Coarse, It Is!

Why did the banana wear sunscreen at the beach?
It refused to peel.

What do you call it when a grain of sand loses its train of thought?
A grain-fart.

How do beaches greet each other?

With a sand-shake.

What do you call a French man who wears sandals to the beach?
Phillipe Phloppe.

What do you call a beach party that gets out of hand?
Sandemonium.

What did one sand dune say to the other?
I will never desert you!

What do sheep wear to the beach?
A baa-kini.

St Patrick's Day

What do you get when you cross poison ivy with a four-leaf clover?
A rash of good luck!

What do you call a fake Irish diamond?
A shamrock!

What instrument does a showoff play on St. Patrick's Day?
Brag-pipes

When is an Irish Potato not an Irish Potato?
When it's a French Fry

Knock, knock.
Who's there?

Erin.
Erin who?
Erin as fast as I could, but I couldn't catch the leprechaun.

When does a leprechaun cross the street?
When it turns green!

How can you tell if an Irishman is having a good time?
He's Dublin over with laughter

March Madness

Why did the college basketball player sign up for the crafting class?
He wanted to learn how to make baskets!

How do NCAA basketball players stay cool during a game?
They stand near the fans.

Why don't they hold NCAA tournament basketball games in the jungle?
Too many cheetahs.

Why do referees carry mops during March madness tournament basketball games?
Because there's so much dribbling.

Why do basketball players eat donuts?
They love to dunk them.

Why was Cinderella thrown off the Syracuse basketball team?
She ran away from the ball.

Easter

Why did the Easter egg hide?
Because it was a little chicken!

What do you call a rabbit who tells jokes?
A funny bunny!

Why did the Easter egg hide?
Because it was a little chicken!

What do you call a rabbit with fleas?
Bugs Bunny!

What do you get if you pour boiling water down a rabbit hole?
Hot cross bunnies!

How do you catch a unique wabbit?
U 'neek up on it.

How do you catch a tame wabbit?
Tame way, U 'neek up on it.

Memorial Day

Why did the soldier go to art school?
He wanted to draw his own battle plans!

How did the military chef greet everyone on Memorial Day?
With a hearty "grill-ten-hut!"

Why did the flag go to therapy?
It was feeling a little "pole"-arized!

What did the soldier say to the ocean on Memorial Day?
"Thanks for all the "sea"-rvice!"

Why did the soldier bring a ladder to the picnic?
Because they heard they needed to "raise the stakes" in horseshoes!

Juneteenth

Juneteenth is a significant and solemn occasion, commemorating the emancipation of enslaved African Americans in the United States. While it's important to recognize and honor the historical significance of Juneteenth, it may not be appropriate to make jokes about it.

Instead, I encourage you to learn more about the history of Juneteenth, reflect on its importance, and consider ways to actively support and uplift the community.

Summer

Why did the sun go to school in the Summer?
To get brighter!

What do you call a snowman with a suntan?
A puddle!

Why don't oysters share their pearls in the Summer?
Because they're shellfish!

What do you call a seagull that flies over the bay in the Summer? A bagel!

Why did the tomato turn red during the Summer?
Because it saw the salad dressing!

Independence Day

Why did the British army go to the bakery on Independence Day?
They wanted to get a slice of America's freedom cake!

What do you call a patriotic insect?
A "firecracker"!

Why did the flag bring a sunscreen to the Fourth of July party?
It didn't want to get 50 shades of red, white, and blue!

What did one flag say to the other flag?
"Nothing, it just waved!"

Why did the fireworks get a ticket?
They were caught speeding on the Fourth of July!

Autumn

Why did the scarecrow win an award?
Because he was outstanding in his field!

What do you get when you drop a pumpkin?
Squash!

Why did the leaf go to the doctor?
It was feeling green!

How do trees get on the internet?
They log in!

What did one autumn leaf say to another?
I'm falling for you!

Labor Day

Why did the scarecrow get a promotion on Labor Day?
Because he was outstanding in his field!

What do you call a worker who loves spicy food?

A labor of "heat"!

Why did the worker bring a ladder to the Labor Day picnic?
To reach the highest level of relaxation!

How did the skeleton celebrate Labor Day?
He worked his fingers to the bone!

Why did the computer go on strike on Labor Day?
It wanted better "byte" and working conditions!

Employment

When an employment application asks who is to be notified in case of emergency, I always write, "A very good doctor".

I can't believe I got fired from the calendar factory.
All I did was take a day off.

I'm great at multitasking.
I can waste time, be unproductive, and procrastinate all at once.
If it wasn't for the last minute, nothing would get done.

I get plenty of exercise – jumping to conclusions, pushing my luck, and dodging deadlines.
I asked the corporate wellness officer, "Can you teach me yoga?" He said, "How flexible are you?" I said, "I can't make Tuesdays."

What do you call that day when you finally do all the chores and work you've let pile up?
Tomorrow

A farmer's career criminal son was supposed to be helping him with the chores but when he looked behind the barn, he was asleep on the hay.
He was out on bale.

Veterans Day

What do you call a Veteran who survived mustard gas and pepper spray?
A seasoned Veteran!

Why don't scientists trust atoms?
Because they make up everything, just like our brave veterans!

How do you thank a veteran?
With a big salute and a heartfelt "thank you"!

Why did the soldier bring a ladder to the Veterans Day parade?
Because they wanted to reach new heights of honor and respect!

What do you call a veteran who can play the guitar?
A "strumming soldier"!

Thanksgiving

Why aren't turkeys hungry on Thanksgiving?
Duh, they're already stuffed.

What do you say to the winner of the corn-shucking contest?
Corn-gratulations.

How can you unlock the greatest Thanksgiving experience ever?
By making sure to bring the tur-key

What kind of 'tude is appropriate at the family dinner?
Gratitude.

Why didn't the pilgrim want to make the bread?
It's a crummy job.

When are turkeys the most grateful?
The day after Thanksgiving.

Why was the turkey asked to join a band?
He could bring his own drumsticks.

What do you call rain on Turkey Day?

Fowl weather.

What did dad say when he was asked to say grace?
Grace.

Did you hear the one about the rude turkey?
It was jerky.

Winter

Why did the snowman bring a broom?
Because he wanted to sweep the competition!

What do you call a snowman with a six-pack?
An abdominal snowman!

What do you get if you cross a snowman and a vampire? Frostbite!

Why did the bicycle fall over in the snow?
Because it was two-tired!

How do snowmen get around?
They ride an "icicle!"

Why are winter days great?
They're snow much fun!

What do snowmen call their kids?
Chill-dren.

What is a snowman's favorite snack?
Ice-krispies treats.

What is a snowman's favorite drink?
Iced tea.

What is a snowman's favorite dinner?
Brrrrrritos.

Knock, knock.
Who's there? Scold. Scold who? [It']Scold outside!

Knock, knock.
Who's there? Icy. Icy who? Icy you!

Christmas

Why did the Christmas tree go to church?
Because it wanted to get "tree"-ligious!

What do you get if you cross a snowman and a vampire? Frostbite!

How do angels greet each other during the holiday season?
Halo, halo, halo!

Why did the gingerbread man go to church?
He wanted to find some "holy" icing!

What did the wise men say to each other while following the star?
"We're really star-struck!"

Why did Santa go to music school?
Because he wanted to improve his "wrap" skills!

How does a snowman get around?
By riding an "icicle"!

Why did the Christmas tree go to the barber?
It needed a trim (to look "tree-mendous" for the holiday season)!

Why did Santa's helper see the doctor?
Because he had low "elf" esteem!

Why did the gingerbread family go to therapy?
They had too many unresolved cookie issues!

What did one snowman say to the other snowman?
"Do you smell carrots?"

How does Santa keep his suits wrinkle-free?
He uses Claus-tarch!

Why did the Christmas ornament go to school?

It wanted to get an "ornament-al" education!

Why did Mary and Joseph use a donkey to travel to Bethlehem? Because it was their way of "mule-ing" over the hills and through the valleys!

How do angels greet each other during the holiday season?
They say, "Halo there!"

Why did the wise men bring gifts of gold, frankincense, and myrrh?
Because they couldn't find a good deal on Amazon!

Why was the math book sad during the holiday season?
Because it had too many "problems" to solve!

Why did the shepherds bring a ladder to the nativity scene? Because they heard the angels were "high" above!

What do you call a snowman with a six-pack?
An "abominable" snowman!

Why did the scarecrow go to church?
Because it heard it needed some "serious" prayer!

What do you call a snowman with a Bible?
Frosty the Believer!

How does Moses make his coffee?
Hebrews it!

Why did the angel go to school?
To improve its "halo "gram!

What carol do they sing in the desert?
"O Camel Ye Faithful"!

HAPPY

It might seem crazy what I'm about to say
Sunshine she's here, you can take away
I'm a hot air balloon, I could go to space
With the air, like I don't care baby by the way

Because I'm happy
Clap along if you feel like a room without a roof
Because I'm happy
Clap along if you feel like happiness is the truth
Because I'm happy
Clap along if you know what happiness is to you
Because I'm happy
Clap along if you feel like that's what you wanna do

Here come bad news talking this and that
Yeah, give me all you got, don't hold back
Yeah, well I should probably warn you I'll be just fine
Yeah, no offense to you don't waste your time
Here's why

Because I'm happy
Clap along if you feel like a room without a roof
Because I'm happy
Clap along if you feel like happiness is the truth
Because I'm happy
Clap along if you know what happiness is to you
Because I'm happy
Clap along if you feel like that's what you wanna do

Happy, bring me down
Can't nothing, bring me down
Love is too happy to bring me down
Can't nothing, bring me down
I said bring me down
Can't nothing, bring me down
Love is too happy to bring me down
Can't nothing, bring me down
I said

Because I'm happy
Clap along if you feel like a room without a roof
Because I'm happy
Clap along if you feel like happiness is the truth
Because I'm happy
Clap along if you know what happiness is to you
Because I'm happy
Clap along if you feel like that's what you wanna do

Because I'm happy
Clap along if you feel like a room without a roof
Because I'm happy
Clap along if you feel like happiness is the truth
Because I'm happy
Clap along if you know what happiness is to you
Because I'm happy
Clap along if you feel like that's what you wanna do

Happy, bring me down
Can't nothing, bring me down
Love is too happy to bring me down
Can't nothing, bring me down
I said

Because I'm happy
Clap along if you feel like a room without a roof
Because I'm happy
Clap along if you feel like happiness is the truth
Because I'm happy
Clap along if you know what happiness is to you
Because I'm happy
Clap along if you feel like that's what you wanna do

Because I'm happy
Clap along if you feel like a room without a roof
Because I'm happy
Clap along if you feel like happiness is the truth
Because I'm happy
Clap along if you know what happiness is to you

Because I'm happy
Clap along if you feel like that's what you wanna do

Songwriter
PHARRELL L WILLIAMS

Published by
Lyrics © Peermusic Publishing, Sony/ATV Music Publishing LLC,
Warner/Chappell Music, Inc., Universal Music Publishing Group

REVIEW ASK

If you enjoyed this book, please leave a review! Your feedback will help us improve future releases.

I'd also appreciate your honest reviews on Amazon, Goodreads, BookBub, and markcoverton.com.

Let's share God's Word by writing a review about the Assignment! I read all reviews and use your feedback to make future books even better for you.

Amazon.com/author/markoverton

http://www.goodreads.com/author/7647613.Mark_C_Overton

BookBub.com/profile/mark-c-overton

Ask an Authorgraph at https://www.authorgraph.com/authors/goodnewsbookset.

Your reviews matter a lot to us, and we thank you endlessly! On the other hand, the most essential write-up is you yourselves. Your life is a letter written in my heart; everyone can read it and recognize the good work among you. Indeed, you are a letter from Christ showing the result of ministry among you.

READ OTHER BOOKS BY MARK C. OVERTON

"True Words for True Believers"

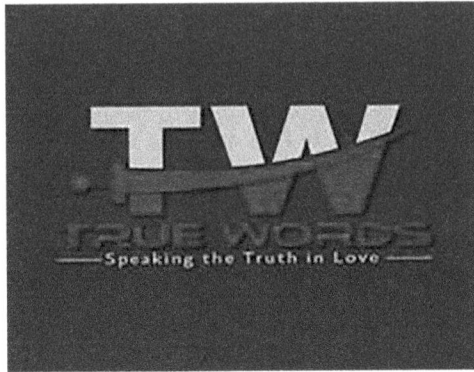

Promises

Win at Work

Church Leader Series

Assignment

Crossroads

Second Editions

Faith Transformation, 2nd Edition

LORD, Teach Me How to Pray, 2nd Edition.

Faith Series

Faith Excellence

Faith Transformation

The Good Book Series

New Day, New Life (Series Compilation)

What Love Really Means

You Only Live Once

I Like to Start with Something Funny

LORD, Teach Me How to Pray

Chapter and Verse

Airmen Series

Career Progression Guide for Airmen: The Basics

Career Progression Guide for Airmen

Faith Builder | Faith Influencer | For Lifelong Faith Followers

DISCOVER BONUS BOOK CONTENT

I can only offer so much in this book, but you can watch trailers for each book at https://youtube.com/@truewordsalways. The world of social media has exploded in recent years because of story. The power of story can connect and motivate people to be further involved in each other lives and to care for and have compassion for others.

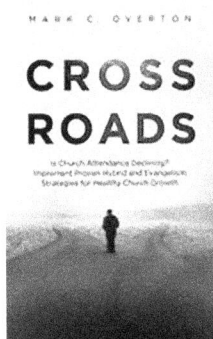

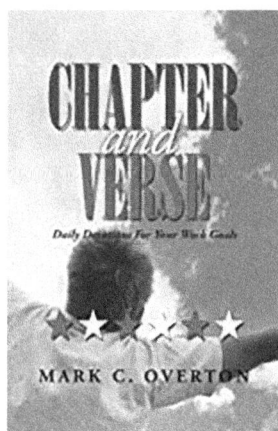

www.ingramcontent.com/pod-product-compliance
Lightning Source LLC
Chambersburg PA
CBHW032055040426
42335CB00037B/813